The Higher Civil Service
in Europe and Canada

Brookings Dialogues on Public Policy

*The presentations and discussions at Brookings conferences and seminars
often deserve wide circulation as contributions to public understanding
of issues of national importance. The Brookings Dialogues on Public Policy
series is intended to make such statements and commentary available
to a broad and general audience, usually in summary form. The series
supplements the Institution's research publications by reflecting
the contrasting, often lively, and sometimes conflicting views of elected
and appointed government officials, other leaders in public and private life,
and scholars. In keeping with their origin and purpose, the Dialogues
are not subjected to the formal review procedures established for the
Institution's research publications. Brookings publishes them in the belief
that they are worthy of public consideration but does not assume
responsibility for their accuracy or objectivity. And, as in all Brookings
publications, the judgments, conclusions, and recommendations
presented in the Dialogues should not be ascribed to the trustees, officers,
or other staff members of the Brookings Institution.*

The Higher Civil Service in Europe and Canada
Lessons for the United States

Papers by BRUCE L. R. SMITH

WILLIAM PLOWDEN

COLIN CAMPBELL, S.J.

RENATE MAYNTZ

BERNARD GOURNAY

JAMES W. FESLER

DAVID T. STANLEY

HUGH HECLO

*presented at a conference
at the Brookings Institution
on June 23–24, 1983*

Edited by BRUCE L. R. SMITH

THE BROOKINGS INSTITUTION
Washington, D.C.

Library of Congress Catalog Card Number 84-070254
ISBN 0-8157-7991-7

9 8 7 6 5 4 3 2 1

About Brookings

THE BROOKINGS INSTITUTION is a private nonprofit organization devoted to research, education, and publication in economics, government, foreign policy, and the social sciences generally. Its principal purpose is to bring knowledge to bear on the current and emerging public policy problems facing the American people. In its research, Brookings functions as an independent analyst and critic, committed to publishing its findings for the information of the public. In its conferences and other activities, it serves as a bridge between scholarship and public policy, bringing new knowledge to the attention of decisionmakers and affording scholars a better insight into policy issues. Its activities are carried out through three research programs (Economic Studies, Governmental Studies, Foreign Policy Studies), an Advanced Study Program, a Publications Program, and a Social Science Computation Center.

The Institution was incorporated in 1927 to merge the Institute for Government Research, founded in 1916 as the first private organization devoted to public policy issues at the national level; the Institute of Economics, established in 1922 to study economic problems; and the Robert Brookings Graduate School of Economics and Government, organized in 1924 as a pioneering experiment in training for public service. The consolidated institution was named in honor of Robert Somers Brookings (1850–1932), a St. Louis businessman whose leadership shaped the earlier organization.

Brookings is financed largely by endowment and by the support of philanthropic foundations, corporations, and private individuals. Its funds are devoted to carrying out its own research and educational activities. It also undertakes some unclassified government contract studies, reserving the right to publish its findings.

A Board of Trustees is responsible for general supervision of the Institution, approval of fields of investigation, and safeguarding the independence of the Institution's work. The President is the chief administrative officer, responsible for formulating and coordinating policies, recommending projects, approving publications, and selecting the staff.

Contents

vii

Contents

Editor's Preface

THIS volume grew out of a Brookings conference held on June 23–24, 1983, attended by scholars and practitioners from Europe and North America, on the higher civil service. The conference and book were made possible by a grant from Sydney Stein, Jr., Chicago investment adviser, philanthropist, and Honorary Brookings Trustee, who saw the need for a fresh examination of the subject. The book is dedicated to him in the hope that the ideas presented here will advance his vision of excellence in the public service.

I gratefully acknowledge the assistance of my Brookings colleagues James L. Sundquist, Gilbert Y. Steiner, A. Lee Fritschler, James M. Mitchell, David T. Stanley, Walter E. Beach, A. James Reichley, and Herbert Kaufman in planning the conference, commissioning the papers, and thinking about the problems facing the higher civil service today. Colin Campbell of Georgetown University, Hugh Heclo of Harvard University, James W. Fesler of Yale University, Alfred Diamant of Indiana University, Ezra Suleiman of Princeton University, Edie Nan Goldenberg of the University of Michigan, and James D. Carroll of Syracuse University were also particularly helpful. Rosslyn S. Kleeman of the General Accounting Office provided encouragement and advice. George Nesterczuk of the Office of Personnel Management kindly gave me the benefit of his views on civil service reform.

The contributors to the volume were a delight to work with, and I will cherish my association with them. Each of us benefited from the intelligence, good humor, and informed judgment of the other conference participants. The public servants from the United States and other countries who attended the conference were especially stimulating.

Donna J. Roginski edited the manuscript; Nancy Snyder proofread it; and Alex P. Orfinger provided editorial assistance. Maxine R. Mennen coordinated arrangements for the conference and assisted in the preparation of the manuscript.

Washington, D.C.   BRUCE L. R. SMITH
February 1984

The U.S. Higher Civil Service in Comparative Perspective

BRUCE L. R. SMITH

IN JANUARY 1983, on the centennial anniversary of the Pendleton Act, the civil service system created by that statute seemed in deep crisis. The signs of trouble were numerous. Surveys reported poor morale among senior executives. A high percentage of eligible career officials were retiring early, and it was becoming more difficult to recruit gifted young people into public service. Political attacks on the bureaucracy and its real or imagined ills were rampant.[1]

This was also the year in which the U.S. Office of Personnel Management (OPM) was to present to Congress a review of the Senior Executive Service (SES) established by the Civil Service Reform Act of 1978, perhaps the most important piece of civil service legislation since the Pendleton Act itself. Although the statutory provision mandating the OPM report was invalidated by a Supreme Court ruling,[2] the need for an assessment of the 1978 act was widely acknowledged, and the administration announced its intent to proceed with the review despite the ruling.

1. James L. Perry and Lyman W. Porter, "Organizational Assessments of the Civil Service Reform Act: Second-Year Report—Executive Summary" (University of California at Irvine, Public Policy Research Organization, October 1981); James L. Perry and Peter S. Ring, "Reforming the Upper Levels of the Bureaucracy: A Longitudinal Study of the Senior Executive Service: An Interim Report" (Washington, D.C.: NAPA, October 1981); Patricia W. Ingraham and Peter W. Colby, "Political Reform and Government Management: The Case of the Senior Executive Service" (State University of New York at Binghamton, Center for Social Analysis, October 1981); Elmer B. Staats, "Governmental Performance in Perspective: Achievements and Challenges," in Bruce L. R. Smith and James D. Carroll, eds., *Improving the Accountability and Performance of Government* (Brookings Institution, 1982); National Academy of Public Administration, Panel on the Public Service, "The Senior Executive Service: An Interim Report" (Washington, D.C.: NAPA, October 1981); and Mark A. Abramson and Sandra Baxter, "Evaluating the Civil Service Reform Act of 1978: A View from One Department (Washington, D.C.: Council for Excellence in Government, 1983).

2. The case involved the "legislative veto," that is, the practice whereby administrative action can be vetoed by a concurrent resolution in one or both houses of Congress and in some cases by committee action. The Supreme Court held in *Immigration and Naturalization Services* v. *Chahda* (51 U.S.L.W. 4907) that such actions were violations of the constitutional requirement that the president must approve, and has veto powers over, congressional enactments.

Thoughtful observers, in brief, feared for the future of the civil service system, especially in the senior ranks that are so important to policy formation. The hard-won gains of constructing an able career service that helped the nation through the turbulent period of the Great Depression, World War II, and postwar reconstruction seemed in danger of forfeiture. The Brookings Institution, aided by a grant from Sydney Stein, Jr., a Chicago investment adviser, philanthropist, student of America's governing institutions, and a Brookings honorary trustee, decided to convene a conference to assess the current state of the higher civil service in the United States. The conference's aim was to explore ideas for reform through a look at the experiences of other industrialized nations. This volume presents the results of the conference, and the present chapter sketches the framework within which the individual contributors sought to grapple with the issues.

In deciding to look at how other nations organize, staff, and manage the higher civil service, we were aware both of the shrill quality of a domestic debate that often casts problems in exaggerated form and of the nostalgia for parliamentary systems that sometimes afflicts our own critics. Nonetheless, the conference organizers believed that much could be learned from a careful examination of how the higher civil service works in other industrialized nations.

From afar it may appear that European nations have evolved civil service systems that function with less clamor, confusion, and jarring discontinuities. European career officials may seem better integrated into the governing system, either because of an agreed doctrine on their role or, perhaps more likely, because long usage and custom have shown that civil servants are a natural part of managing society's business. The papers presented here explore the detailed workings of the higher civil service systems of Great Britain, Canada, the Federal Republic of Germany, and France, and are written by experts from each of the countries named. The papers seek to follow a common format, insofar as that is practical; they discuss the relationship between higher civil servants and political officials, the patterns of mobility for careerists, the role of specialist and generalist traditions, the internal governance of the civil service, and executive development and training practices. Each contributor also gives his or her overall assessment of the achievements as well as the shortcomings of the system. The conference organizers also invited experienced senior practitioners from each country, along with a number of scholars, political appointees, and career executives from the United States.

The aim was to produce a stimulating mix of perspectives to aid the dialogue on the problems of the public service in America.

While we cannot claim to have produced any definitive solutions, our hopes for a useful exchange of views were amply fulfilled. This volume testifies to our modest faith that understanding how others have coped with common problems may provide a measure of practical guidance in the conduct of our own affairs. Even if no such ready application of ideas and practices from other nations were possible, we have achieved at least a deeper awareness of the range of choices available to us, of the complexity of the linkage between the polity and the wider culture, and of the subtleties of the myriad roles that the public servant is called upon to perform in a modern democracy.

Administrative capacity and historical tradition

One objective of the conference was "to determine if the impression of greater administrative capacity in Europe is warranted and, if so, what could be learned for the American context." This proved to be an elusive goal. If by administrative capacity one means the ability to set clear policy goals, then the French and German systems might be said to possess such capacity. The two systems also appear to be able to implement program goals, though this is less self-evident than their ability to set planning targets. French successes in program implementation, as discussed in Bernard Gournay's paper and elsewhere, include productivity improvements in industry, assistance for economic growth, civilian nuclear power, transportation infrastructure, oil policy, and regional development.[3] Other programs in France have produced average results (for example, in welfare, health care distribution, and education) or have remained only pronouncements (for example, the fight against inflation, foreign worker programs, fiscal reform, and campaigns against alcoholism and for road safety). It goes without saying that along with the ability to set goals and design programs goes the chance of dramatic failure (the Concorde) or even scandal (the reconstruction of the Villette slaughterhouse in Paris). German programs at the federal level are more in the nature of broad program goals, since implemen-

3. See Bernard Gournay's paper in this volume; Jean-Luc Bodiguel and Jean-Louis Quermonne, *La Haute fonction publique sous la Vième République* (Paris: Presses Universitaires de France, 1983); and Ezra N. Suleiman, *Politics, Power, and Bureaucracy in France: The Administrative Elite* (Princeton University Press, 1974). Valuable comparative studies are Joel D. Aberbach, Robert D. Putnam, and Bert A. Rockman, *Bureaucrats and Politicians in Western Democracies* (Harvard University Press, 1981); and Colin Campbell, *Governments under Stress: Political Executives and Key Bureaucrats in Washington, London, and Ottawa* (University of Toronto Press, 1983).

tation and program management in most policy areas rest with the state, or *Länder,* governments.

Nonetheless, the contrasts with the United States are manifold. The disjunction between policy goals and the capacity to achieve them, the slippage in translating policy into program, and the tendencies toward confusion and overlap of functions at the operating levels of government seem markedly greater in the United States. The disconnection between career and political levels is partly responsible. Politicians formulate policies without involving the career civil servants who will implement them, and careerists pursue programs without lining up the requisite political support.

As a random sampling of massive program failure, consider President Kennedy's effort to involve the poor in the implementation of various poverty programs, President Johnson's community economic development programs and "showcase" educational assistance efforts, President Nixon's attempts at regional population redistribution, and President Carter's policies toward children.[4] In all these cases closer involvement by high-level career officials in policy formation and greater political awareness by civil servants would have averted misunderstandings and better served the nation's interests.

Clearly, however, the higher civil service is only one part of a complex system. Legal and constitutional structures, political parties, interest group activities, the political culture, attitudes toward authority, and many other factors influence the outcomes of policy debate and shape the government's capacity to implement decisions. Thus, even if one could achieve agreement on the criteria for program success, the effort to assign relative weights to one or another factor in shaping the outcome is problematical. Of course, the policymaking and implementation process is so complex that examples and counterexamples can be arrayed endlessly, making judgments about the capacities of the whole system difficult. The conference participants agreed it was im-

4. James L. Sundquist, *Dispersing Population: What America Can Learn from Europe* (Brookings Institution, 1975); Sundquist, "A Comparison of Policy-Making Capacity in the United States and Five European Countries: The Case of Population Distribution," in Michael E. Kraft and Mark Schneider, eds., *Population Policy Analysis* (Lexington Books, 1978); Gilbert Y. Steiner, *The Futility of Family Policy* (Brookings Institution, 1981); Jeffrey Pressman and Aaron B. Wildavsky, *Implementation* (University of California Press, 1973); George R. LaNoue and Bruce L. R. Smith, *The Politics of School Decentralization* (Lexington Books, 1973); and Daniel Patrick Moynihan, *Maximum Feasible Misunderstanding* (New York: Free Press, 1970).

possible to trace policy successes or failures back through the process to determine the administrative capacities of the various systems.

Administrative capacity as a concept is too amorphous, the actions of civil servants too embedded in the total institutional context, and the programs of administrative agencies too varied to allow a satisfactory assessment of higher civil service performance according to some uniform standard of measurement. The higher civil services in the various countries are called upon to perform different functions, and each ultimately must be judged in its own terms. The French and German higher civil services operate within a tradition of strong executive authority and thus function differently from those in Britain and Canada, where there is a strong parliamentary tradition. Historically, parliamentary authority in Britain came before the bureaucratic state, and this has had its impact on the modern civil servants who assist ministers in dealing with Parliament as the primary preoccupation of their jobs. The necessity to hold one's policies up to rigorous scrutiny and to submit to lengthy parliamentary debate seemingly constrains somewhat the administrative official's scope for action. But at the same time, it builds consensus, leads to the orderly articulation of interests, and facilitates the task of gaining acceptance of public policies. The parliamentary system in Britain, and the even greater involvement of legislators in policy formulation in the United States, may sacrifice a measure of speed and coherence, but it gains administrative capacity through public acceptance of governmental action. Yet since the Crown has its prerogative powers, British administration has a different cast from that of the United States, where all administrative authority derives from legislative action.

The American administrative system, moreover, seeks representativeness as a goal more than the European systems do. This is because Americans believe that a representative civil service promotes the wider ends of political legitimacy and stability, qualities of great importance in a large, heterogeneous nation. There can be no capacity in a system lacking a broad base of public support. But, as our European colleagues assure us, there is no need for Americans to take a defensive posture and to justify our civil service system merely by reference to broader ends. Considered in the more narrow terms of management skills, personnel issues, the use of modern information systems, and the like, the United States has achieved some enviable results. (All of our systems, however, have serious defects that need to be remedied, especially in the area of training and executive development. These issues will be addressed later.)

The American emphasis on management as opposed to policy derives from historical tradition. The modern large-scale business enterprise is a great American innovation. The British invented the institution of Parliament, and the continental Europeans gave birth to nation-states with strong executive apparatuses that came out of the old monarchies, but the United States in the nineteenth century created the large-scale business enterprises that transformed the worlds of commerce, industry, and transportation.[5]

Since business management antedated the rise of government bureaucracy, it was natural that the framers of the civil service system should look to business models. The U.S. civil service system was thus a mixture of the desire for representativeness, the urge for business efficiency, and the determination to put an end to the abuses of patronage.[6] The American idea of merit in civil service was based as well on a misunderstanding of the British civil service reforms that followed the Northcote-Trevelayn inquiry of 1854. To the Americans, merit meant qualifications for a specific position as measured by competitive examination; merit was to be shorn of any bias in favor of a cultural elite. The British understood merit in the at once looser yet more demanding sense of "fitness to govern." As a result the British competitive examination process has produced a disproportionate number of candidates from precisely the cultural elite so distrusted by the U.S. civil service reformers.

*Working
assumptions*

While eschewing universal standards for administrative performance, and while cautioning that the process of social learning across different cultures often includes the misreading of others' experiences, the conference participants reached broad agreement on a few neutral principles of good civil service practice. These assumptions provide a point of departure for a more detailed examination of different civil service strategies for recruitment, training, internal governance, political involvement, and other

5. Alfred D. Chandler, Jr., *The Visible Hand: The Managerial Revolution in American Business* (Harvard University Press, 1977).

6. Paul P. Van Riper, *History of the United States Civil Service* (Evanston, Ill.: Row, Peterson, 1958), chap. 5; Herbert Kaufman, "The Growth of the Federal Personnel Service," in Wallace S. Sayer, ed., *The Federal Government Service* (Englewood Cliffs, N.J.: Prentice-Hall, 1965), pp. 7–69; and William E. Nelson, *The Roots of American Bureaucracy, 1830–1900* (Harvard University Press, 1981).

issues. The propositions, partly descriptive and partly exhortative in character, can be loosely stated as follows:

1. The general esteem in which the civil service is held affects performance. Political attacks on the civil service have wide ramifications and invite a rapid deterioration in the quality of the public service.

2. The quality of people in the higher civil service, and the performance of civil servants throughout the ranks, are measurably improved if a few career people achieve positions of high political power, either appointive or elective, and if high-level policymaking routinely involves at least some senior civil servants.

3. Career staff should be allowed to participate early on in the policymaking process. No one has ever found a useful, practical distinction between "policy" and "management," or between "substance" and "detail." Cabinet ministers, chiefs of state, and political and appointive officials are engaged along with career civil servants in a seamless web of activity that involves the endless weighing of means against ends and ends against means. All have a share in formulating, implementing, and selling public policies to citizens.

4. The complete political neutrality of the higher civil service is a polite fiction, and strict adherence to it clouds thought. Politicians should be entitled to have some say in choosing their closest career aides, provided that their intervention in the process of assignment and promotion is done lightly and within some generally understood rules. The basic professionalism of the career service can be reconciled with high-level policy involvement.

The troubles of the U.S. civil service begin to be seen clearly with reference to the first of the above assumptions. Political attacks on the civil service in the United States have helped cause widespread demoralization among career officials in recent years. A milder version of the same problem recently has been evident in the United Kingdom, where, despite high unemployment, the government failed to fill a number of entry-level posts that are normally considered highly desirable. Higher civil servants in the United States have also seen themselves blocked off from effective participation in policymaking by a new layering of political appointees in many departments and central staff agencies. Furthermore, the opportunities to rise through the ranks into the higher reaches of political authority have gone from rare to practically nonexistent.

The American civil servant was once a more serious participant in policy formulation than he or she is today. But nothing in our experience has resembled the French practice of civil servants serving in cabinet posts (at one point 40 percent of former President Valéry Giscard d'Estaing's ministers were civil servants) or the strong British reliance on civil servants in framing issues for policy choice. However, the dominant role of the civil servant in Britain and Canada, accompanied by the myth of complete political neutrality, has created strains in both nations. Such strains are less evident in France and Germany, where the relations between career and political officials have been more openly dealt with. The United States has suffered the worst of both worlds, seeming to embrace in contradictory fashion both the view that career officials are too political (and therefore cannot be trusted by a new administration) and the notion that they are mere technicians who should have nothing to do with policy.

Before proceeding further with the analysis, we should set some boundaries and definitional limits for the inquiry.

Classifying higher civil service positions

Table 1 presents in simplified fashion the civil service posts in each country that are the focus of our attention. James W. Fesler, in his contribution to the volume, examines the differences in the national systems and spells out the implications of the contrasting practices. For our present purposes, we need note only a few points.

First, there are substantially larger numbers of political appointees in the American system than in the European systems. Putting aside the question of scale, the United States clearly has more political appointees in subcabinet positions than any of the other nations examined here. Furthermore, in the United States political appointees reach farther down into the government hierarchy. In the United States the deputy assistant secretary is frequently a political appointee while his counterpart official in Europe is almost invariably a career civil servant.

Second, the exact place to draw the line between career and political positions in the United States is not always clear. Practices vary widely across the civilian agencies.

Third, special corps such as the Foreign Service, the Federal Bureau of Investigation, the Internal Revenue Service, the Public Health Service, the Agricultural Research Service, the Food and Drug Administration, and a number of others depart from the simplified picture presented in the diagram. The practice in these agencies approximates the pattern found in Europe of careerists occupying positions up to and sometimes including the highest subcabinet posts. The complexity and variety of U.S. practice complicates the analysis, and makes simple comparisons between the American and the European systems difficult. The problem in comparing higher civil service posts is apparent when we recall such positions are more likely to be defined in the United States in terms of specific task-oriented skills and professional training.

The focus of our attention is on higher-level positions of a broad management and policy-advisory character where politics and administration meet within the large civilian line departments and the few major staff units serving the president. We are concerned only secondarily with such staff specialities as lawyers, economists, statisticians, and scientists, although we recognize that occasionally these individuals may influence broad policy and that agencies dominated by such specialists constitute a larger share of total governmental activity in the United States than in Europe.

The national security and foreign policy establishments in each

Table 1. *Higher Civil Service Positions in the United States, Canada, France, Germany, and the United Kingdom, 1982*

United States	United Kingdom	Canada	Germany	France
Secretary	Minister	Minister	Minister	Minister
Deputy secretary	. . .[a]	. . .[a]	. . .[a]	. . .[a]
Under secretary	Permanent secretary	Deputy minister	Staatsekretär	Secrétaires-génèraux
Assistant secretary (500 Executive I–V positions and 800 other appointive positions)	Second permanent secretary	Associate deputy minister and senior assistant deputy ministers	Ministerialdirektor	Directeurs-génèraux, directeurs and conseillers d'état, and préfets
Deputy assistant secretary[b]	Deputy secretary	Assistant deputy minister	Ministerialdirigent	Sous-directeurs
. . .[a]	Under secretary	Director-general	Ministerialrat	Administrateurs civils
Chiefs, directors, and so on	Assistant secretary	Director	. . .	. . .
7,500 SES positions (10 percent political, 90 percent career)	2,000 positions	2,200 positions	1,700 positions	4,000–5,000 positions
Addendum: Total national government civilian work force				
2,800,000	526,000	220,000	332,000	2,200,000

a. Career positions are below this line.
b. This position and those below are part of the Senior Executive Service (SES).

country are excluded to simplify the task of analysis. While the national security and the foreign policy arenas exhibit national differences, these are less marked than the contrasts between the civilian civil service traditions of Europe and America. The bipartisan aura, the influential role of professionals, and the special complexities of civil-military relations give a distinctive cast to policy processes in the national security field that deserves separate treatment.

The positions belonging to the Senior Executive Service consist of the approximately 7,500 positions established under the Civil Service Reform Act of 1978. This act and subsequent decisions created a category of officials that included most of the senior careerists in the former General Schedule (GS) 16 to 18 ranks, plus many subcabinet appointive positions. (The highest level appointive officials defined under the Executive I–V Schedule and some other appointive positions established by various statutes remain outside the SES.) It is not the intent of this or any paper in the volume to conduct a full review of the 1978 Civil Service Reform Act, but it must be noted that, like the major reform of the British civil service attempted after the Fulton Report of 1968 and like recent French efforts to widen access to the Ecole Nationale d'Administration (ENA), the U.S. effort has not fundamentally altered the nature of the civil service system. The 1978 act sought to create a corps of higher civil servants with broad experience who could serve in a variety of posts across the government and who would be subject to more stringent performance standards in return for the potentially greater rewards accompanying superior performance. But greater interagency mobility has not been achieved, nor has there been an adequate test of the incentive pay feature. Congress significantly reduced the funds available for merit bonuses, and in the general atmosphere of fiscal stringency, the compensation of high-level civil servants has been subject to an overall limit imposed by law. But the important point for our purposes is that the essential features of the old system remain: the heavy reliance on political appointees at the subcabinet level; the tendency for these "public careerists"[7] to have short terms in office; the modest opportunities for late or lateral entry into the civil service, as opposed to strict progression through the ranks; the penetration by legislators and their staffs into executive

7. The term is borrowed from Hugh Heclo, "In Search of a Role: America's Higher Civil Service," in Ezra N. Suleiman, ed., *Bureaucrats and Policymakers: A Comparative Overview* (New York: Holmes and Meier, 1984). See also Hugh Heclo, *A Government of Strangers* (Brookings Institution, 1977).

policymaking and the details of administration; and careers mainly within a single department. These broad system features, in comparison with the institutions and practices adopted in the United Kingdom, France, Germany, and Canada, form the central focus of our inquiry.

Relations between careerists and political appointees

The United States has had greater difficulty both in devising a theory and in establishing effective working relationships between career and political officials than the other nations reviewed in this volume. While the dealings between career and political officials can be marked by contention and strife even in France and Germany (as explained in the papers by Bernard Gournay and Renate Mayntz), their relationship, in a phrase coined by one of the conference participants, is one of "conflictual stability." There is wrangling, sometimes public but more often behind the scenes, and a good deal of heat; yet all parties understand the rules of the game, and the conflict does not spill over into the kind of acrimony that would jeopardize the system.

Yet there are some interesting differences between the French and the German systems. The Germans, alone among the nations examined, have a formal mechanism whereby a cabinet minister can involuntarily retire the state secretary. This mechanism, which applies only to the highest level of career official, is based on the recognition that the higher civil servant inevitably plays a role in defending administration policies. The French practice is more informal, relying on complex understandings that apply to the political behavior of career officials. Some career civil servants are "party political" (clearly identified with and loyal to a particular party); others are politically sensitive while not directly identified with a political party; still others conform more to the image of neutral competence. The French have some difficulties resulting from poor communication and their traditional avoidance of face-to-face conflict. But by and large the subtle customs that apply to the various types of political behavior are understood, and the system functions without the paralyzing disputes that emerge within the American "government of strangers." Ultimately, both the French and German practices are sustained by tradition. Even the formal German device of involuntary retirement has its roots in the *politische Beamte* (political official) role of the higher civil servant in Prussia 150 years ago.

Britain and Canada have had more difficulty in achieving a stable, consensual relationship between career and political officials. A root cause of the difficulty, as discussed in the papers by

William Plowden and Colin Campbell, lies in the rigid adherence to the doctrine of political neutrality among civil servants. Still, on this point the participants from Britain and Canada did not reach full agreement: the academics tended to believe that an incoming government must be allowed more discretion in choosing top career officials while the practitioners tended to support the status quo. The problem is perhaps illustrated most dramatically in Canada. After nearly forty years of unbroken Liberal party rule, almost all higher civil servants were closely identified with that party. Yet astonishingly, in the brief nine-month break in Liberal party rule, only three officials—aside from ministers—were replaced by Prime Minister Joe Clark. (He was, however, on the brink of a large-scale shakeup when his government collapsed.)

The Canadian practice of virtually no turnover other than at the highest political levels stands at one end of the spectrum; the American practice of wholesale replacement of policy officials, with ripple effects throughout the career ranks, stands at the other. Wholesale changes in the ranks of civil servants are not limited to the federal level in the United States. In some state and municipal jurisdictions the entire administrative staff is, in effect, subject to the appointment powers of an incoming governor or mayor. While it would be hard to argue that either the state of Pennsylvania or the city of Chicago is less well governed than comparable units of government elsewhere in the nation, the disadvantages of turnover on this scale are apparent, not the least in the drain on the chief executive's time and energy.

An effective modern administration seems to require something between the near-absence of turnover and the massive replacement of the top layers of government. A new administration needs to be able to appoint subcabinet officials in order to feel comfortable and confident of its capacity to carry out an electoral mandate. Selecting sympathetic career people for sensitive posts would be partly, but not wholly, a substitute for the appointment of loyal outsiders. One reason why there should be fewer outsiders than has been the case for recent American presidents is that it is difficult to make discriminating judgments about several thousand appointees. The large number of appointive officials, many of whom will be pursuing agendas of their own, complicates the task of policy coordination. The Reagan administration has been cautious in filling subcabinet posts because of its reported concern with finding ideologically compatible appointees. It is, perhaps, an ironic straw in the wind that an American administration suspicious of the federal civil service should point the way toward greater reliance on career officials working in tandem with a smaller and more select group of appointees to accomplish broad policy changes.

Internal governance and career mobility

If incoming governments seek a voice in the job assignments of senior civil servants, will serious harm be done to the integrity of the system? How, in fact, do other nations regulate the careers of higher civil servants? Total autonomy based upon a strong central personnel agency apparently does not exist. None of the national systems examined has a tradition of a strong central personnel agency. The Germans come close to having a highly regulated civil service, but this is through a body of law enforced by the courts in the tradition of the *Rechtsstaat* rather than through any central agency. The British for a time attempted to have a strong civil service department, but Prime Minister Thatcher disbanded it, blaming the department for a civil service pay agreement she disliked and fearing that it would come to represent the guild interests of officials.

The normal situation is for a weak coordinating mechanism, a committee or staff agency, to be combined with powerful departmental influences or the influence of a specialized professional corps. The higher civil service nowhere seems to think of itself as a unified guild but rather as a fragmented cluster of departmental or professional groups. Political influence resembles, from the agency perspective, other external forces that affect career lines. Indeed, an admixture of political influence in directing civil service careers might help to create broader perspectives and wider loyalties. Political involvement, in the sense of an active interest by policy-level officials in improving the service and in nurturing the professionalism of its members, does not need to have a destructive influence on the higher civil service. Neglect and indifference are more serious dangers. Political influence, if exercised in a reasonable fashion and with the knowledge and understanding of the senior civil servants, can serve the broad interests of the career service as well as the policy requirements of an incoming administration. The recent destructive political attacks on the civil service in the United States and elsewhere should not blind us to the continuing need for dialogue and mutual accommodation among politicians and civil servants.

Because the central mechanisms are often so weak, the career patterns of higher civil servants generally reflect little mobility outside the departments in which they first entered government service. In Britain, except for a very few officials who reach the highest career rank of permanent secretary, careers are made within a single department. There is great mobility within the department but little across departmental lines. Canada has done somewhat better, with a greater degree of lateral entry in high-level civil service positions and with somewhat more movement between departments. Still, most careers are within a department, as is also the case in Germany. France stands alone among the nations reviewed in the conference in having a high degree of career mobility across departments and in the movement of officials between the public and the private sectors. The integrative mechanisms that exist in the French system—mainly the elite educational institutions that serve as gates of entry and the seven professional corps that to a degree oversee careers—facilitate such movement. The American "public careerist" displays mobility, but the process is marked by happenstance, the constraints of conflict-of-interest laws, personal hardship, and jarring discontinuity in policy. The conference participants agreed that for most of our countries a great deal more should be done to plan for an orderly career progression for higher civil servants.

Executive development and training

All of the countries examined, with the possible exception of France, lack effective career development mechanisms to assist the men and women whose potential impact on national policies is significant. Even in France the individual civil servant pursues an atomistic course propelled largely by personal ambition, friendships, and the shifting tides of bureaucratic and political fortune. Lip service is paid to the goals of careful career planning and to training efforts, but few countries have developed effective programs. There is a need to take seriously the training and career-development dimension of the higher civil service.

No single formula, however, can serve the needs of the varied systems. In Germany the legal training of most higher civil servants needs to be supplemented with the techniques of policy analysis and empirical research skills. In Britain the challenge is to devise a substitute for the random short-term rotations that used to be regarded as the best imaginable sort of training and are now the object of widespread criticism. The United States has devoted more thought and effort to post-entry and mid-career training programs than have European nations, but the problems of course design, of appropriate timing, and of motivating senior civil servants to take time away from operational responsibilities for themselves or for their subordinates continue to pose severe challenges. The need for more and better training cannot be a mere incantation; it must be felt and understood by those for whom such efforts are designed.

Political executives, too, can benefit from better preparation for their jobs. The parliamentary tradition, with a shadow opposition government waiting in the wings, provides to some degree a cadre of thoroughly briefed officials with knowledge of their departments. But for junior ministers, and especially for the large number of political appointees in the American system, the transition to a position of high executive responsibility can be a shattering experience. Training programs tailored for the political executive may play a constructive role.

A much more controversial matter in executive development strategies is the role of a formal performance appraisal system. None of the nations represented at the conference has found a satisfactory means of appraising the performance of senior government executives, much less a system that closely links pay with performance evaluations. Canada had for a time a performance evaluation system closely linked to pay incentives, but the plan was suspended in a climate of fiscal austerity before it had a chance to operate. The U.S. performance pay system called for in the Civil Service Reform Act has suffered a similar fate, although merit bonuses on a reduced scale have been paid. Periodic reviews of performance by superiors exist in all of the civil service systems discussed. But as one moves up the ranks to the highest levels of responsibility, the criteria for performance are increasingly difficult to establish. The incentive pay systems of industry, more heavily oriented toward quantitative measures and usually tied to the company's market performance, seem problematical in the public service context. The paraphernalia of performance appraisal that has evolved in the United States since the 1978 act has become a nightmarish triumph of form over function.

Specialist versus generalist tradition

A final theme is the contrast between specialist and generalist traditions in the U.S. and the European civil service systems. Generally speaking, the civil services of Europe (less so for Canada, which is closer to the United States in this respect) encourage the rise of generalists to the higher ranks, while in the United States higher civil servants typically have specialist backgrounds. There is less here than meets the eye, however. The above generalization turns out to have limited utility in understanding the differences between the American system and the others, or in pointing the way toward reform. For the most part, the individuals who reach the higher ranks in America are no longer specialists in any meaningful sense of the term. Policymaking inevitably involves the blending of skills and knowledge from a variety of specialized backgrounds. Attacks on the amateurs or generalists, as in the Fulton report in Great Britain, miss the point as much as do the critical assaults on the alleged narrowness of U.S. career officials. The point is that higher civil servants, in order to perform the job, will have to become "specialists in generalization" and approach the task from a perspective broader than what is commonly understood as specialization. At the same time, this broad perspective does not preclude—indeed, it often demands—learning a great deal about numerous specialized subjects. A good case can be made for purging the specialist-generalist dichotomy from the vocabulary of public administration.

An alternative formulation advanced recently by Rufus Miles appealed to a number of conference participants.[8] Miles divides modern government into a cluster of related mission areas, such as national security and foreign policy, health and human services, procurement, research administration, contracting, income transfer programs, regulatory activities, and the like. Higher civil servants would function within one or another of these program clusters, serving as policy advisers or program managers within a framework broader than the traditional single department but more focused than the entire range of government activity. He dismisses as a myth the idea that a manager or policy adviser can function equally well in all the diversified operations of modern government. Still remaining is the difficult task of integrating the broad program clusters and of working out the treaties that govern the behavior of agencies at the jurisdictional boundary lines. Much of the work of the SES falls in this latter category and requires integrative capacities transcending even the multi-agency perspective suggested by the clusters.

A special problem that exists with certain functional specialities in each nation merits further examination. The problem involves the lawyers, scientists, accountants, statisticians, economists, and others (the exact categories differ slightly from country to country) who perform indispensable, and indisputably specialist, functions. Even within these specialist groups, the path to promotion lies in the managerial and the more generalist skills. Promotion typically is available only to those who supervise the work of their peers.

8. Rufus E. Miles, Jr., "Rethinking Some Premises of the Senior Executive Service," in Smith and Carroll, eds., *Improving the Accountability*.

This means that the best technicians are often forced into a managerial career path or, alternatively, out of the public service into more lucrative careers in the private sector. In all the countries examined here, the universities, private industry, law firms, accounting firms, and other private employers seem to have done a better job than government of retaining the talented young professionals (though government can often attract good young lawyers, statisticians, and the like for an initial period of service).

This failure to provide attractive long-term career opportunities frequently results in government research laboratories, general counsels' offices, statistical bureaus, and other specialized units becoming professional backwaters. The tradition of the senior scientist in industry, the full professor in the university, and the partner in the law firm, where pay and perquisites are available to the senior professional and to the manager in at least somewhat more equal measure, has not been adequately developed in government. The need for professional satisfaction for this group of higher civil servants is reinforced by their only peripheral involvement in broad policy issues (though there may be considerable variation from agency to agency in the policy role of these specialists).

Future directions for the United States

The lessons to be drawn for the United States from this review of European experience seem deceptively simple in some respects. Yet the answers to the fundamental questions remain elusive. As David Stanley notes, the American higher civil service would clearly benefit from restraint on the part of those politicians who have launched partisan attacks on it. In recent years the U.S. higher civil service also appears to have suffered from neglect and underuse. It may strike the European reader as odd to hear of civil servants being "frozen out" of policy discussions; a more familiar complaint to their ears is likely to be the politician treated cavalierly by the clever civil servant (as in the shenanigans portrayed in the British television show, "Yes, Minister"). At any rate, one way to restore morale among higher civil servants would be to guarantee that they have a voice that is heard in the inner councils of policy.

A more controversial step is to rely on more career and fewer appointive officials in subcabinet and other high-level positions. This would not be a total departure from past practice and would resemble the pattern found in the national security and foreign policy areas and in some civilian U.S. agencies that have strong career traditions. To move in this direction would remedy some of the problems with the large number of appointive officials who move in and out of government. This group brings energy and innovative capacity to our governing system, but it also brings confusion, discontinuity, disorderliness, and amateurism. Another idea is to reserve some key subcabinet posts for career people, tempering or even reversing the informal presumption that the plums go to appointees and the hardship assignments to careerists. This flexibility is available within the framework of the 1978 act, which specifies only that there be a nine-to-one ratio of careerists to political appointees *government-wide* for all SES positions.

Such proposals make sense and would, for those who derive comfort from being in the company of others, nudge our system a few steps in the direction of what is more nearly the standard practice in other nations. But merely to state the ideas is to run up against the realities that have shaped our system and created its distinctive character. Incoming American administrations want positions for political supporters and campaign contributors. Senior civil servants associated directly with a previous administration are not trusted except in national security, where more or less bipartisan attitudes prevail. Openness, accessibility, representativeness, and power-aversive behavior are more highly esteemed in our civil service tradition than continuity of policy or the influence of a continuing body of experts. Indeed, anything that smacks of such prerogatives is feared.

The lessons we learn from Europe are neither unambiguous nor wholly supportive of the intended changes. Each of the nations reviewed in this volume seems at least vaguely dissatisfied and bent on reform of its own system. Britain and Canada are pondering the potential inclusion of more appointive officials in the higher ranks, or at least a more open role for politicians in the choice of senior civil servants. France has sought to broaden entry into the public service by adding a new category of candidates for the ENA. German reformers want a more representative group of officials, less legalistic and better versed in modern policy analysis. The European reformers, in a sense, want to reform their own systems by incorporating some of the strengths of American practice.

But it seems clear that the problems America faces are of a different order. The continental statist tradition and Anglo-Saxon parliamentarism both proceed from an acknowledged role for the higher civil service in their governing systems. The changes they seek are at the margins; there exists no doubt that a modern democracy requires civil servants; long usage leads to unconscious acceptance. It is only a slight exaggeration to say that they have no need for theory.

For Americans, as Hugh Heclo shows in his concluding commentary, the problem is deeper. If we truly wish a role for a permanent higher civil service, we will have to devise a doctrine to justify its place in our constitutional system of limited powers. If we want the civil service to be more than a collection of nonpolitical technicians operating at the fringes of the policy process, we will have to redirect the role of the political party; to alter the expectations of the campaign worker; to redefine the lines of authority between the cabinet secretaries, the president, and career officials; and to clarify the premises underlying congressional and interest group involvement in decisionmaking within the executive branch. We will also have to educate, recruit, train, and manage the careers of public servants better than we have done. The nation has long been deeply suspicious of any kind of permanent establishment. The framers of the Pendleton Act were more concerned with representativeness than with other values. In their view, the civil service system could be made open and accessible to all persons of talent if government service were defined in terms of concrete, operational tasks rather than in terms of a broader concept of fitness to govern, which might allow an elite to monopolize power. It was a system designed to manage and not to govern. The latter task was to be left to a relatively few elected officials and to other citizens who occasionally would be called upon to serve in high office. For us to make a place for a higher civil service will require an examination and restatement of fundamental premises. We will have to make the case that policy continuity and disinterested public service at the higher levels of government can be reconciled with the underlying values of our large, diverse, and disorderly democracy.

The Higher Civil Service of Britain

WILLIAM PLOWDEN

TWO POINTS should be made at the beginning of this paper. First, the British higher civil service, in its present form, has several major characteristics that sharply distinguish it from the American civil service. These characteristics have changed remarkably little in the past fifty years. Second, these characteristics, the circumstances that encourage them, and the administrative style that they are believed to engender are now under sustained criticism from outside the service and intensive discussion within it. As a result, the British higher civil service may well change in the next decade or so.[1]

The British higher civil service has long been marked by several distinctive characteristics: it is typically a lifetime career occupation; as a whole, it is virtually autonomous in matters of staff selection, movement, promotion and discharge; it encourages and is built around the skills of the generalist rather than of the specialist; and its members are fully involved in virtually all aspects of policymaking, however sensitive. Indeed, the British higher civil service dominates policymaking to the virtual exclusion of all but a small number of senior elected politicians.

Certain other features follow from these. The higher civil service is middle-aged (in the sense that senior posts are very rarely held by young people). It is an elite, and is therefore isolated, physically and culturally, from the community at large. It believes strongly in the right of government to govern, but its outlook is dispassionate and, in political terms, centrist.

Definitions and statistics

In Britain the term *civil servant* excludes categories of people who in other countries are included: employees of public corporations and of the National Health Service, school teachers, police, and so on. Broadly speaking the term refers to the staff of some

1. The opening sections of this paper draw heavily on the valuable factual accounts given in several papers by Professor F. F. Ridley, published together as *The British Civil Service: Recruitment, Promotion, Remuneration, Politics* (University of Liverpool, 1983).

eighteen to twenty central government ministries plus such agencies as the Stationery Office, the National Savings Department, and the Royal Mint. Excluding industrial civil servants (for example, workers in defense factories), there were in 1982 some 526,000 civil servants. Of this total about 40 percent belonged to the administration group, which embraces at one end clerks, typists, and other junior unskilled grades and, at the other, general administrators at the heads of departments. This group is paralleled by other specialist groups up to senior levels. A few specialists—senior scientists, for example—have wide managerial responsibilities. But the subgroup that is most important for the conduct of government business as a whole consists of the 450 or so general administrators in the "open structure" (the top three grades) plus about 1,000 senior members of the administration group. These administrators are usually also the policymakers, so the distinction between the two, which is one of the subjects of the Brookings conference, is not as important in Britain as it is elsewhere.

This paper will focus on this key group of fewer than 2,000 people. Two qualifications should be made. First, many of the rules governing their conditions of service are common to many other officials outside the group. Second, officials outside the group form part of the pool from which some recruits to the group are drawn.

The legal framework

The Crown—that is, the executive—regulates and controls the civil service in Britain. The Crown's prerogative powers are independent of Parliament and are refined by an "order in council." Parliament thus has no formal powers over the structure of the civil service nor over the conditions under which civil servants are employed. (However, legislation is needed to create or abolish departments, and there is a formal limit on the number of salaried cabinet ministers.)

Recruitment and promotion

Until the second half of the nineteenth century, civil service posts were among the main prizes in a long-established spoils system. Reforms enacted then created an independent Civil Service Commission to oversee recruitment, which was to be by competitive examination. Today lower-level appointments (90 percent of the total) are made by individual departments according to rules laid down by the Civil Service Commission. The commission itself directly appoints recruits to the administrative trainee (AT) grade, which is the gateway to the highest offices.

Applicants for AT posts from outside the civil service must be between twenty and twenty-seven years old. (Arrangements are occasionally made for older candidates.) They must have a degree from a university or its equivalent. Applicants from inside the service may be between twenty-one and thirty-one years old; they too must have a university degree or two years of service.

The first stage of the entrance competition consists of written examinations. The 10 to 15 percent of candidates who pass then undergo two days of written and oral tests and interviews; they are asked to deal with case studies and to take part in and lead group discussions.[2] Those who pass this hurdle then undergo an extended individual interview conducted by a final selection board composed of the head of the Civil Service Commission, two civil servants, and two non-civil-service members. In recent years about two-thirds of all successful candidates have been from outside the service, mostly new university graduates. Some 20 to 40 percent have been women.

AT candidates apply for the department(s) of their choice. Depending on their personal qualities, performance in interviews, individual preferences, and the positions available, they will be assigned to a particular department. Though the significance of this is administrative rather than legal, the first posting largely determines the course of a new official's subsequent career. The rules and conditions that govern civil service careers are laid down centrally, but the actual administrative implementation is delegated to individual departments. The Management and Personnel Office (MPO), headed by a senior minister who reports to the prime minister, acts as civil service "management" in dealings with civil service staff (who are represented in important matters by several civil service unions). Three major concerns, however, are beyond the jurisdiction of the MPO: questions of civil service pay, numbers, and pensions are left to the Treasury. Between 1968 and 1982 all these matters were the responsibility of the Civil Service Department.

Within the centrally determined rules, individual personnel departments have great freedom in managing the careers of departmental staff, at least for most grades. Ministers normally take little interest in determining the general policy on postings and promotions, still less in the movements of individuals. (The very top posts are an exception.)

2. The second stage of the examination process was originally derived from, and still resembles, the procedures used by the War Office Selection Board during World War II and later to select large numbers of temporary army officers.

The typical senior administrator begins his career at the AT level, where variety and versatility are the key words. An administrator destined for the top is shaped as a generalist in subject-related skills and as a specialist (or so the boast goes) only in the peculiar techniques of working for ministers. Working mainly within the department to which he or she was first posted, the trainee will move between posts with widely varying content. He or she may stay between two and four years at the AT level, with postings lasting between a few months and a year. Thereafter, the civil servant is likely to spend between two and three years in each post until the ceiling is reached. In 1977 the average tenure of assistant secretaries or under secretaries in one large department was two and one-half years; it was even shorter in the Treasury— only one and one-half years. A 1971 study found that among bureaucrats who had served an average of twenty-three years, fully two-thirds of those who had risen fastest to the top had held eleven or more different posts.[3]

The men and women who are believed to have real potential are moved around rapidly and are given experience in one or more of the key posts that are felt to broaden and test people: private secretary to a junior or senior departmental minister or, for a few, to the prime minister; or positions in the cabinet secretariat, the Treasury, or perhaps the British delegation to the European Commission in Brussels. In 1980 eighteen of the twenty-three permanent secretaries had served in either the Treasury, cabinet offices, or the prime minister's office. The successful administrator shows himself able to handle any task with equal skill and aplomb: finance or personnel work, negotiation, piloting draft legislation through Parliament, drafting speeches, writing minutes and, above all, advising ministers.

These "high flyers" move between departments, especially at the very senior levels. Most administrators, however, spend most of their careers in the same department; a 1971 study showed that just over half of senior officials with an average of twenty-nine years of service had worked in a ministry other than their current one.[4] These figures probably reflect movements brought about by departmental reorganization and, in particular, by the disappearance during the 1960s of the old Colonial Office. A small proportion of senior officials spend a short period outside the civil service altogether, on secondment to a merchant bank, an industrial

3. Peta Sheriff, *Career Patterns in the Higher Civil Service* (Her Majesty's Stationery Office, 1976).
4. Ibid.

corporation, the National Health Service, or a local authority. (In 1982, 102 civil servants spent some time in business and commerce.) The same 1971 study found that about a quarter of those in the open structure had spent a year or more outside Whitehall, though only 12 percent of this group had spent as much as a quarter of their adult life in another activity.

Selection for the administration group depends on general academic qualifications and on having passed the selection process. Promotion depends on performance in the requisite range of jobs; it does not depend on having or acquiring specific qualifications, nor on completing prescribed training. Promotion rates are partly influenced by the annual staff reports made on all civil servants. These are written by a civil servant's immediate superiors, whose own superior checks, countersigns, and comments on them. The form used is standard in all departments for all grades from clerical officer to assistant secretary. All officials also have annual job appraisal interviews with officers two levels up from their own. These interviews allow for frank dialogues about individual performance, needs, hopes, and prospects.

Up to the level of assistant secretary, an individual's career is left to his or her department. Above that, the top three grades are linked in the open structure, all of whose members are in principle eligible to fill posts in any department at the appropriate level. Procedures for promotions within the open structure are neither codified nor published; broadly, nominations from the MPO and the department concerned are discussed in an interdepartmental committee of permanent secretaries, whose recommendations are approved by the prime minister. (This last step is normally a mere formality.) In practice most open structure posts below permanent secretary are filled from within the department in question. Permanent secretary posts are the exception. Appointments here are made after discussion in the same interdepartmental committee, but also after consultation between the head of the civil service and the ministerial head of the department. Once again the prime minister is consulted. This stage is much less of a formality than in the case of the lower ranks; it is quite clear that Mrs. Thatcher in particular has decisively influenced the choice of several recent permanent secretaries. At this level there is a good deal of movement between departments; in a sample of the most recent group of new appointments (1982–83), several had made their careers in or come from a department other than that which they were now appointed to head.

Training

A recent civil service report summarized the three main types of skills required of civil servants: strategic skills, needed for advising ministers on policies and for planning and implementing the policies; managerial skills, required to manage people, money, and other resources; and skills in more specialized areas like accounting, personnel work, automatic data processing, and so on.[5] Of these, strategic skills have traditionally been seen as by far the most important. Yet these are also the skills that are least easily gained by formal training.

By the standards of the past, a lot of attention has been paid to training since the late 1960s, when the central Civil Service College was created. (Some 90 percent of all training is still carried out within departments for their own staff.) Every AT is expected to undergo at least sixteen weeks of induction training during his first two years; but after this, the amount and type of training received will depend on a mixture of chance and personal choice. Departments have a great deal of discretion in this regard. Though the Management and Personnel Office can, through the Civil Service College, provide some training centrally, it cannot require departments to send their staff to such courses. There are no mandatory requirements for staff to complete certain courses before filling certain posts or reaching certain senior levels in the service. The true high flyer is, if anything, likely to receive less training than his more pedestrian colleagues, since his time can less easily be spared. Moreover, even in the civil service of the 1970s and 1980s, many of the high flyer's superiors will not take seriously his training needs, since few of them have been trained themselves or have been shown the importance of training. Most entrants will have had about six months formal training by the time they become principals. In 1981–82 the average *annual* amount of management training undergone by all staff at the level of senior principal and above was half a day.

Conditions of service

Civil servants have no special rights to their jobs. Though their careers are normally for a lifetime, especially in the senior grades, this is a matter of custom rather than of right. Civil servants may be dismissed for inefficiency or misconduct, although in practice such dismissals are very rare.

Old and well-organized staff associations and trade unions

5. *Civil Service Management Development in the 1980s* (Management and Personnel Office, 1983).

represent the major groups in the civil service—administrators, scientific and technical personnel, clerical and ancillary staff, and so on. Nine such associations jointly represent civil servants in negotiations with management (as drawn from the Treasury and the MPO) in a consultative body known as the Civil Service National Whitley Council. For many years the Whitley Council successfully resolved issues without industrial strife. In the last few years, however, increased militancy among the associations and tougher management policies, particularly on pay, have led to sharp disagreements and, in 1981, to a long and costly strike. (There are no formal prohibitions against strikes in the civil service.) The future of the Whitley system thus seems uncertain. Meanwhile, regulations for the day-to-day behavior of civil servants (governing everything from the circumstances in which they may buy first-class rail tickets to their participation in political activity) are laid down in an evolving loose-leaf document known as the Estacode.

Pay issues are so important and have become so contentious in the recent past that they should be examined briefly here. Rates of pay for each grade are the same throughout the service. With some exceptions (including the top three grades of the open structure), annual salaries within the rate for a grade rise by between 4 and 11 percent annual increments to a ceiling. There is also an annual pay settlement that applies equally to all grades in the civil service; this is often a percentage increase that reflects changes in the cost of living. (The open structure grades and their analogues in the technical groups are not affected since their pay is considered separately.)

For much of this century the principle guiding civil service pay determination has been that of fair comparison with good employers in other sectors. During the 1960s and 1970s, these comparisons were made by an independent pay research unit that reported to the government. Its reports were only advisory, but its recommendations were broadly accepted. The result was that civil service pay rose steadily in line with inflation and with pay increases in the private sector. Equally important, the introduction in 1971 of index-linked pensions gave civil servants a guaranteed hedge against inflation for the rest of their lives. The Civil Service Department's success in getting this "bonus" from the Treasury was one reason why Mrs. Thatcher wanted to abolish the department in order to control the costs of the central bureaucracy.

The arrangements described above were suspended during the late 1970s, when the Labour government tried to impose an incomes policy on all sectors of the economy; they were scrapped altogether in 1981 by Mrs. Thatcher's government in its attempts to cut salary bills throughout the public sector. The Thatcher government set up a review panel on civil service pay headed by a senior judge. After hearing a great deal of testimony, the panel concluded that more weight should be given to market forces in determining civil service pay levels; that comparisons should play a smaller part than in the past; that independent management consultants should collect and analyze the data required; that in making comparisons with private sector firms, more weight should be given to smaller undertakings (which generally pay less well than large ones); and that in all but the top grades pay should be related to performance.[6]

Skills and life chances

In a cabinet system, the interests of the departments are represented by their ministers around the cabinet table, in Parliament, on television, or in public speeches. The skills traditionally most esteemed among civil servants are those necessary to help ministers to perform these tasks. (The same skills are, of course, even more important in the prime minister's office.) The apt answer to the parliamentary question, the aggressive yet noncommittal speech, the emollient negotiating brief to deal with a difficult delegation, the appropriate concession to resolve an impasse on a draft bill, even the record of the cabinet discussion that gives the prime minister's summing-up rather more bite and direction than it in fact had, are all examples of achievements that are highly valued and that can help to secure promotion. All are highly political in the sense that they are essential elements in the process of bargaining and persuading, whether within government or in public. It follows that the distinction between policy and administration is even more meaningless in the activities of the higher civil service than it is elsewhere, since all senior civil servants are liable to find themselves intimately involved in the overlapping processes of planning, devising, modifying, and selling policy.

In this context the importance of the administrator is enhanced by two factors. First, in his dealings with his specialist colleagues in the civil service, the generalist administrator is unquestionably in the lead. Specialist groups—be they economists, scientists, statisticians, lawyers, or researchers—are advisers, not managers; their lines of communication with the policy process, and with

6. Sir John Megaw, chairman, *Inquiry into Civil Service Pay,* cmnd. 8590 (HMSO, 1982).

ministers, are lateral, via the generalist administrators. Though some specialists may have managerial roles in their own special areas—for example, senior scientists in running scientific research establishments—their work is outside the mainstream policy process. There are exceptions to this rule—military professionals in the Ministry of Defence, and, occasionally, senior economists in the Treasury. But on the whole, important policies are made by generalists in the administration group; specialists may be involved, but usually only in advising administrators in circumstances determined by the latter. Although 40 percent of open-structure posts are held by people from specialist areas, these are essentially specialist posts. The most certain route to key positions in general management still is direct entry to the AT grade at an early age; few top administrators have been promoted from lower grades within the service or have been late entries from other walks of life. It is broadly typical that of the six permanent secretaries profiled in the appendix, only one (Sir James Hamilton) should have started his civil service career outside what is now the administration group. It is also typical that none should be a woman: there are no female permanent secretaries, and only four deputy secretaries and twenty-five under secretaries. Atypically, two of the new appointments are less than fifty years old.

The second reason the administrator remains important and influential is that in Britain career civil servants have managed, to an extent rare in similar governmental systems, to retain a virtual monopoly of the key positions within government. There are only two potential groups of competitors: the "in-and-outers" with specific professional skills and political sympathizers appointed by the government of the day. Both groups are small. The tradition is well established that an incoming government makes very few, if any, changes in the distribution of civil servants among posts, however sensitive; nor will an individual minister make many changes when replacing another as head of a ministry. There have been occasional discreet changes of permanent secretary and, slightly more often, of private secretary, but these are the exceptions. In the past prime ministers have brought advisers of their own choice into government with them, and in the last decade or so it has become common for departmental ministers to bring in one or two personal aides. But the scale of such political appointments is minuscule; more important, to date such appointments have been made only to advisory and not to line management positions.

It follows from the above that the personal fortunes of individual officials are rarely affected by changes of administration. Even in an area as politically contentious as industrial policy, the same senior officials (including the permanent head) have continued to serve at the Department of Industry under a Conservative government, its Labour successors, and now the present Conservative government.

Current criticisms

Almost every aspect of the system described here has been extensively discussed and criticized in the past few years. Criticisms start with the selection procedures. Long-standing objections from the political left have focused on the social and educational origins of the higher civil service, especially the apparent bias shown in favor of the private schools and Oxbridge. The objective facts are beyond dispute: in all recent years up to the present, a high proportion of new ATs have come from outside the civil service (typically straight from university) rather than from inside via internal promotions; they have had middle-class backgrounds and have been educated in private schools and at Oxford and Cambridge; they have studied the humanities rather than the natural and social sciences. In the 1960s this class-related critique was given added impetus by the argument that senior officials who had studied nontechnical subjects at university were not competent to staff a government intent on creating a new industrial revolution. The conclusion was that more civil servants should be recruited from the working class and from science-based universities. The recruits should be more expert, less amateur. In 1965 a committee of the House of Commons studied the civil service recruitment process. It concluded that the structure, the skills and capabilities, and the public image of the service needed improvement and modernization.[7] Its report led to the appointment of a governmental committee of inquiry chaired by Lord Fulton. In his 1968 report, Fulton argued that the civil service was outdated in structure, style, and culture, and that it was incapable of dealing with the problems of the modern world.[8] Fulton was extremely critical of the generalist tradition:

> The ideal administrator is still too often seen as the gifted layman who, moving frequently from job to job within the Service, can take a practical view of any problem, irrespective of its subject matter, in the light of his knowledge and experience of the government machine. . . . The cult is obsolete at all levels and in all parts of the service.[9]

7. *Recruitment to the Civil Service,* Sixth Report from the Estimates Committee, 1964–65, House of Commons 308 (HMSO, 1965).

8. Lord Fulton, chairman, *Report of the Committee on the Civil Service, 1966–68,* cmnd. 3638 (HMSO, 1968).

9. Ibid., vol. 1, paragraph 15.

The solution to the problem, Fulton said, was for new entrants to have university degrees that related more closely to the work they were to do, for their careers to be managed so that they developed specialized skills (very broadly divided into economic-financial and social), and for them to receive much more training. (A new Civil Service College was to be set up to encourage this.) Fulton also criticized the class structure of the civil service; he objected both to the rigidity of the divisions between different levels in the same hierarchy and the divisions between different types of skills or professions. Both contributed to maintaining the senior administrators as an isolated priesthood. Fulton wanted to abolish both sets of boundaries and to create a unified grading structure that would allow good people of whatever background to compete freely for posts and to move easily within the service.

Fulton suggested that the career professionalism of the civil service should be modified by encouraging more movement in and out at all levels, and that steps should be taken to make the service more representative of the nation at large by broadening the social base of recruitment. Finally, in arguing for more professional management of the civil service as a whole, Fulton recommended that the personnel function should be taken away from the Treasury (where it had always been located) and given to a new Civil Service Department, which "could fight, and be seen to be fighting, the Treasury on behalf of the civil service."[10]

Following the Fulton report, the Civil Service College and the Civil Service Department (CSD) were set up. The top three administrative grades were merged in the open structure. The previous three administrative, executive, and clerical classes were brought together in a single administration group. These institutional changes suggested that Fulton's proposals were being taken seriously. So they were, by some people. But in practice, despite these changes and a great deal of activity on the part of the new CSD, the basic character of the civil service changed little in the next decade. Oxbridge-educated generalists continued to dominate the civil service; the very top posts continued to be the preserve of those who had made their careers wholly within the administration group. My earlier description of the civil service in the 1980s shows how little Fulton's reforms affected one of the world's most sophisticated bureaucracies.

The years of the CSD were probably the highwater mark of civil service control over its own internal management. Govern-

10. Ibid.

ments took little interest in the matter, apart from periodic ineffectual exhortations to reduce manpower; civil servants themselves determined the conditions under which they were employed. Parliament took only an intermittent interest in these matters.

But governmental interest in civil service management took a quantum leap when the Conservatives came to power in 1979. Prime Minister Thatcher took an unprecedented interest in senior civil service appointments, and the government's determination to cut the size and the cost of the civil service—along with the rest of the public sector—led to some major changes both in formal arrangements and in the working relationships between some ministers and their departments.

As a result there was a new critique and a new response. An early government announcement that the CSD would be abolished (as having done all too good a job in fighting the Treasury and in securing good terms for civil servants) generated much articulate opposition, and action was withheld. But only months later, in November 1981, the CSD was abolished virtually overnight and its two top officials were sent into premature retirement. Its functions were divided between a new Manpower and Personnel Office and the Treasury. The drive for efficiency was expressed in the rather crude form of a targeted 14 percent cut in civil service positions (102,000 posts) in the five years to May 1984, and, rather more subtly, in the establishment of a series of efficiency reviews in all the major spending departments. The reviews were to be conducted by an adviser brought in from the private sector, and their main purpose was to reduce costs in general and manpower in particular by cutting out unnecessary activities and functions. One leading cabinet minister, Michael Heseltine, attracted much publicity by encouraging the development within his large department of a new management information system aimed at increasing ministerial control over the deployment and use of civil service manpower.[11]

These developments derive from and reflect the distinctive philosophy of the Conservative government, but many of them command wide nonpartisan support. A report by an all-party parliamentary select committee on "efficiency and effectiveness in the civil service" favored many of the developments and echoed a number of Fulton's conclusions.[12] It criticized the skills and

---

11. Andrew Likierman, "Management Information for Ministers: The MINIS System in the Department of the Environment," *Public Administration,* vol. 60 (Summer 1982).

12. *Efficiency and Effectiveness in the Civil Service: 3rd Report from the Treasury and Civil Service Committee,* House of Commons 236 (HMSO, 1982).

attitudes of senior administrators as well as some aspects of civil service personnel management. Throughout its general comments on the use of resources ran a thread of criticism of the apparent weakness of the center in relation to the departments. Although acknowledging that individual ministers were responsible for the efficiency and effectiveness of their own departments, the committee urged that "the Treasury and MPO in their relations with individual departments should move away from guidance to prescription without delay. . . . The MPO should do more than has been done in the past to collect examples of good practice in Departments and elsewhere . . . and to disseminate them widely throughout the civil service."

The committee's interest in managerial efficiency also led it to look critically at the way in which senior civil service posts were filled and the way their holders were trained. The committee felt that there was too little career management. Commenting that too few senior officials were interested in management as opposed to policy, the committee recommended that at least some top jobs should be held by people with "successful records in financial and general management"; that the training of line managers should be reviewed and a special staff training course be established for all officials expected to reach deputy secretary or higher; and that ministers should take an interest in the internal workings of their own departments, should establish information systems on the same general lines as Mr. Heseltine's, and should be allowed to change their permanent secretaries if they found that they could not work satisfactorily with them. Many civil servants, as well as government ministers, found most of the committee's proposals acceptable. The government's published reply to the report accepted the recommendations outlined above, though the government saw no need to set up formal arrangements to review the permanent secretaries of the new ministers.[13]

The select committee's report was shortly followed by a much more radical, if superficial, critique. Many civil servants were deeply upset when, in a public lecture in October 1982, Sir John Hoskyns, a former political aide to Mrs. Thatcher, suggested that the moderate, skeptical, and ultimately pessimistic attitude of many officials made them totally unsuitable for radical government. His recommendation was that many more key jobs should

13. *Efficiency and Effectiveness in the Civil Service: Government Observations on the 3rd Report from the Treasury and Civil Service Committee,* cmnd. 8616 (HMSO, 1982).

be filled by political appointees.[14] In a later unscripted television interview, Hoskyns was asked what single step he would take if given the chance to remake the civil service. He replied briskly that he would compulsorily retire everyone over the age of fifty.

The traditional civil service reply to this line of criticism has been that such policies are inappropriate given the nature of politics in general and parliamentary democracy in particular. The primary duty of senior officials, they say, is to follow whatever lead their ministers may give, putting directly into practice the sensible ideas and trying to alert their superiors to the possibly harmful consequences of the less sensible ones. In either case senior officials help cabinet ministers to present their policies and themselves in ways that will not attract damaging criticism from an always vigilant, and often unfair, Parliament and press. Senior civil servants also argue that whatever the case for enhancing the technical and managerial skills of civil servants, it is the ministers themselves who create the continuing demand for the political skills of generalist administrators.

Civil servants and others have also been upset by Prime Minister Thatcher's unprecedented personal intervention in several recent top civil service appointments. Her hand is detected—probably rightly—in the selection of her former (civil service) principal private secretary as permanent secretary at the Ministry of Defence at the unusually early age of forty-eight, and in the choice of an official thought to share her economic views as permanent head of the Treasury. The question that she is said to ask about any person in, or being considered for, a key post is, "Is he one of us?" With Mrs. Thatcher's power enhanced by her party's second victory in the general election of June 1983, civil servants (and some others) are deeply concerned that the future may bring a gradual but significant shift toward greater political influence over civil service appointments in particular and personnel policies in general.

Impressionistic and anecdotal evidence suggests that this and other aspects of the present government's stance toward the public sector bureaucracy is starting to affect both morale and attitudes within the civil service and the service's standing in the outside world. There has been a small but possibly significant number of premature retirements among promising officials in

---

14. Sir John Hoskyns, "Whitehall and Westminster: An Outsider's View," *Fiscal Studies*, vol. 3 (November 1982), pp. 162–72.

mid-career. The failure in 1982 to fill even the limited number (forty-four) of AT vacancies on offer may indicate weaknesses in the selection process, but it may also reveal a lack of enthusiasm for a civil service career that is particularly striking at a time of high graduate unemployment. The 1981 civil service strike was completely unprecedented in scale, in duration, and in the strength of the views expressed on both sides.

The future of the civil service in Britain

Any generalization about an institution as complex as the British civil service must be suspect to some extent, especially in the context of personnel management, since much responsibility is delegated to departments and practices consequently vary. Moreover, what appears to be true of an institution collectively may well be untrue of many of the individuals who compose it. The manifest strengths of the career civil service in Britain include incorruptibility, freedom from partisan influences, and a strongly developed sense of public service. Until very recently, the career civil service attracted so many able applicants for senior posts that it has been able to turn away a large proportion. That being said, though, I believe that there is much validity in at least some of the criticisms made not only during the past few years but over the past two decades. A series of interrelated weaknesses have gone unacknowledged and uncorrected for too long.

A good case can be made for the general administrator, capable of filling a wide variety of posts and applying in each of them the subtle skills required in operating the Whitehall system. But the generalist principle has been used to justify a remarkable lack of coherence in the management of civil service careers and in the fitting of people to posts. Until the present, careers have barely been managed at all, and expertise has been deprecated. Skill in operating the system is valued far more than experience in and understanding of substantive policy areas. Training, and its relationship to experience and to careers, has been equally haphazard. Despite the creation of the CSD and the MPO, too little attention has been paid to personnel management as an activity, still less as a speciality meriting its own expertise. The career principle has been used to justify an absence of mobility between the civil service and other professions, and an insistence, variously formal and informal, on the full lifetime career. The recruitment process reflects the character of the service, and so the new people selected continue to be very much like their predecessors. A large number of talented people fail to apply for civil service posts; others fall at the hurdle of the selection process. Meanwhile, career civil servants have kept a tight grip not only on the policymaking processes within government but also on the personnel management processes which determine who the key policymakers will be. These two factors, combined with the social and professional distance between civil servants and politicians,[15] are probably the main causes of the current lack of confidence, not to say mistrust, now felt by many politicians for civil servants.

All these features of the civil service underlie one of the major characteristics remarked on by critics of all political persuasions: its caution, conservatism, and resistance to change. If the strength of the generalist administrator derives from his political skills, his corresponding weakness is his instinct to avoid the novel or the risky step that could cause trouble. Witness a recent official account of the selection procedures for ATs which describes the exercise that is an important element in the two-day interview process: "The candidates form themselves into a committee, and each in turn takes the chair for the discussion of a problem he or she has been given a short time to study—perhaps an industrial or personnel problem, or some difficulty *liable to cause embarrassment to Ministers or others unless handled sensibly.*" (Emphasis added.)[16] The civil service culture of studied moderation has rarely been more clearly expressed.

As already suggested, the conservatism of the civil service can be perceived in the way it is managed as much as in the advice it gives on policy. This is at least partly due to the sincerely held belief that there is little wrong with existing practices, and that critics do not understand the constraints within which the service has to work. Like other closed professions with strong values of their own, the civil service finds it hard to evaluate the many criticisms made of it, to distinguish the reasonable from the absurd, and to reply effectively to the complaints. I believe that Sir John Hoskyns identified something real and important in his description of senior civil servants as battle-weary pessimists who secretly "do not believe that the country can be saved."[17] But the response of many civil servants to critiques of this kind is simply to dismiss them as the uninformed cavils of outsiders ignorant of the constraints within which civil servants work. It was symptomatic that when the civil service responded to criticisms of

15. In 1971 only 5 percent of British civil servants reported regular contacts with legislators, compared with 64 percent in the United States and 74 percent in Germany.

16. Joel D. Aberbach, Robert D. Putnam, and Bert A. Rockman, *Bureaucrats and Politicians in Western Democracies* (Harvard University Press, 1981), p. 230.

17. Hoskyns, "Whitehall and Westminster."

selection procedures and the apparent bias toward Oxbridge and arts graduates by setting up an enquiry into the subject, it entrusted this to a former permanent secretary, himself an Oxford arts graduate and a member of the panel from which chairmen of the interview boards are drawn. Perhaps not surprisingly the head of the inquiry panel concluded that the "basic structure of the selection arrangements remains sound," and that with some marginal adjustments these could continue to identify "the candidates best suited to the needs of the 1980s and beyond."[18]

It would, however, be unfair not to acknowledge recent internal activity aimed at encouraging more efficient management in the civil service. The comments of the select committee mentioned above have been used as a springboard for developing new practices and new skills. Thus a "Financial Management Initiative" aims to turn today's general administrators into tomorrow's middle managers, officials who can apply newly developed skills to the cost-conscious management of financial and manpower resources within a framework of improved information systems and more thoroughly delegated powers.[19] There are also signs that the civil service is slowly coming to acknowledge criticisms made of the way in which managers are prepared for their responsibilities. An internal report on "management development in the 1980s," published in July 1983, acknowledges the need for greater professionalism and specialization, for more and better-planned training, for more deliberate management of careers, and for more movement in and out of the services at stages other than the very beginning and very end of careers. It suggests that, in general, staff should stay at least three or four years in any post. As a whole, it embodies a tentative shift away from the primacy of the generalist, though its recommendations are still expressed in the diffident tones of a central department with power only to counsel, not to command.[20] The basic philosophy of the report is repeated, succinctly, in the title of a public lecture given in June 1983 by its principal author, the official head of the MPO: "Good managers are made, not born."[21]

A separate report on "Personnel Work in the Civil Service,"

18. *Selection of Fast-Stream Graduate Entrants to the Home Civil Service, the Diplomatic Service, and the Tax Inspectorate; and of Candidates from within the Service,* Report by Sir Alec Atkinson (Management and Personnel Office, 1983), par. 57.

19. *Efficiency and Effectiveness in the Civil Service: 3rd Report.*

20. *Civil Service Management Development in the 1980s.*

21. John Cassels, lecture to the annual conference of the Chartered Institute of Public Finance and Accountancy, Eastbourne.

also published in July 1983, proposed more coherent personnel strategies, more central guidance on personnel matters (and greater delegation of day-to-day work in departments), better internal communication on personnel matters, and more attention to staff management on the part of line officials. It also suggested that in assessments of an individual's performance more weight should be given to actual achievements and less to personal qualities.[22]

Enthusiasm for these developments is not universal, either among civil servants or among politicians. The well-established culture of Whitehall is very slow to change, and many of today's top officials have almost certainly spent too long as administrators to behave now in the way expected of managers. Separate departments are jealous of their independence and are likely to resist any attempts by the MPO to push them too far, too fast, in any particular direction. Many ministers have neither experience nor interest in managing organizations; most ministers probably value too highly the traditional skills of the general administrator to wish to see these replaced among their official advisers by managerial virtues. However, continuing strong interest in all these questions expressed by Prime Minister Thatcher promises to keep them on the active agenda.

This last point is, ironically, almost as much of a threat as a guarantee of success in attempts at civil service reform. The extreme hostility to public sector bureaucracies expressed by the prime minister and some of her senior colleagues is new to Britain, where parties competing for office have rarely, as in the United States, run against the administration. There are three real dangers in this approach. First, it can damage the morale, motivation, and quality of entrants. Second, indiscriminate attacks can change good as well as bad features of the public service. Third, indiscriminate criticism can provoke indiscriminate resistance by those in and around the public service: good as well as bad suggestions may be rejected. It would be a great pity if some much needed reforms were successfully defeated by bureaucratic conservatives as simply being manifestations of Thatcherism.

Lessons for the United States? It is hard to draw conclusive lessons for the administration of one country from the experience of another. The immense gap that separates the American style of staffing from that of most European countries makes such an exercise particularly perilous. Still, the

22. *Review of Personnel Work in the Civil Service,* Report to the Prime Minister and the Lord Privy Seal by Mr. J. S. Cassels (Management and Personnel Office, 1983).

British example suggests several observations that may be relevant. On the positive side, it is worth noting the benefits derived from maintaining the senior civil service as a high-status profession in which all posts up to the very top are open to insiders. Until very recently the British civil service has never been short of high-quality recruits, and it has even been able to turn many good people away. There also has been very little wastage at the middle to senior levels. Well-tried recruitment procedures and arrangements for managing personnel that are, and are known to be, totally independent of political influence have assured the civil service a reputation for honesty and impartiality.

On the negative side, however, the British civil service illustrates by their absence several features that are surely desirable in a modern state bureaucracy: systematic career management, logic in an individual's passage from one post to another;[23] a controlled but significant degree of movement—in both directions—between the civil service and other sectors; better integration of training with career experience and with the promotion of individuals up the hierarchy; a limited and controlled but significant degree of movement of key officials with a change of administration. (The belief that any official is equally suitable to do any job for any administration is as absurd as it is archaic.)

Even harder to act on is the observed need to do something to improve the performance of politicians. Today's insistence on improving management skills among the bureaucracy emphasizes how ill-prepared most politicians are for the tasks they have to carry out as ministers. Their careers as members of Parliament do little to help them to understand either the workings of government in general or of large organizations—such as government departments—in particular. More deliberate preparation for their role—as elected members or chairmen of the board of governmental corporations—should help them in improving the performance of those corporations as a group. This preparation might bring about greater understanding of the bureaucracy itself, and in so doing might reduce the suspicion felt by politicians for civil servants. If so, it could help significantly to improve the uneasy working relationship between the two sides—one of the issues to which this paper, and indeed this conference as a whole, is addressed.

23. There is much food for thought in the proposals outlined by Rufus Miles at an earlier Brookings seminar. See Rufus E. Miles, Jr., "Rethinking Some Premises of the Senior Executive Service," in Bruce L. R. Smith and James D. Carroll, *Improving the Accountability and Performance of Government* (Brookings Institution, 1982).

**Appendix:
Career paths of
six permanent
secretaries**

Ministry of Industry

SIR PETER CAREY (b. 1923): 1945–51, Foreign Office; 1953–69, Board of Trade (later divided into Trade and Industry); 1971–72, Central Policy Review Staff (Cabinet Office); 1972–83, Industry.

SIR BRIAN HAYES (b. 1929): 1956–83, Agriculture; 1983–, Industry.

Ministry of Education and Science

SIR JAMES HAMILTON (b. 1923): 1943–73, Government/aeronautic research establishments; 1973–76, Cabinet Office; 1976–, Education and Science.

DAVID HANCOCK (b. 1934): 1957–59, Board of Trade; 1959–65, Treasury; 1965–66, Graduate scholarship, United States; 1966–72, Treasury; 1972–74, U.K. delegation to the European Community; 1974–82, Treasury; 1982–83, Cabinet Office; 1983–, Education and Science.

Ministry of Defence

SIR FRANK COOPER (b. 1922): 1948–70, Air Ministry; 1970–73, Civil Service Department; 1973–76, Northern Ireland Office; 1976–82, Defence.

CLIVE WHITMORE (b. 1935): 1959–75, War Office; 1977–79, Cabinet Office; 1979–82, Prime Minister's Office; 1982–, Defence.

The Higher Civil Service of Canada

COLIN CAMPBELL, S.J.

MOST countries are bordered by two or more other nations. Canada is no exception. Physically, it lives in the shadow of the most powerful liberal democracy in the world. Emotionally, it clings to the monarchy and parliamentary system it inherited from the United Kingdom. Moreover, within Canada rest two nations, one French, the other English, each distinct in culture, language, and, in large part, geography. You might find these facts banal, but they are at the very root of what makes Canada of interest to this conference. We allow in this gathering that the British, French, and German experiences have something to say to recent U.S. efforts to reform its higher civil service. Canada has stood at the crossroads of influences from the United Kingdom and the United States.

Canada has outgrown both the kid-sister-with-braces image it calls up in American minds and the dependable-oldest-daughter stereotype it conjurs up among Britons. As 25 million people well on their way to taming the world's second largest geographic jurisdiction, Canadians spend much of their time simply building the infrastructure necessary for economic development. Federal and provincial governments, whether of conservative, liberal, or socialist stripe, have undertaken activities that rightists elsewhere would see as the preserve of the private sector. These governments also have entered into partnerships with the corporate world that leftists abroad would view with abhorrence. Bureaucracy in Canada, in a very real sense, has become both big government and big business, with 220,000 people working in the federal civil service under the provisions of the Public Service Employment Act.

This discussion will address four issues surrounding higher civil servants in Canada. These include their involvement in major policymaking activities and forums, their discretion in adminis-tering the service, their recruitment and career routes, and their educational backgrounds and post-entrance training. Along the

40

way, the treatment will assess the degree to which the higher civil service operates as a distinct element of Canada's executive-bureaucratic culture. Space dictates that the discussion focus on the federal government. However, brief references will be made to provincial developments that are harbingers of where some innovations in Ottawa may lead.

The double life of the Canadian mandarin

The genius of the British view of permanent civil servants owes much to the concept that officials simply do the will of their political masters, who, in turn, determine policies on behalf of the Crown while maintaining the confidence of Parliament. As with many constitutional traditions, full assent to the overarching theory demands a great deal of mental agility. In the case of the United Kingdom, an indigenous monarch who is nationally accepted as a symbol of unity maintains at least the illusion of sovereignty resting in and being exercised on behalf of a single person.

Those reaching this level of abstraction find themselves on a verdant plateau, dotted with distinctions pleasing to discerning constitutional tastes. Elections, rather than registering the will of a sovereign people, merely establish periodically the complexion of the body whose confidence ministers of the Crown must maintain. To be sure, ministers must belong to Parliament. However, they need not be elected—that is, they very often are lords. Having assumed their positions, they become members of the government. They don the veil of collective responsibility, whereby their procedures and deliberative institutions, decisions, divergent points of view, and advice received from officials, all remain concealed from the public if that is deemed to be in the best interests of the Crown.

Although the word *obeisance* barely does justice to the external demeanor of permanent officials toward ministers, the former find numerous conventions upon which to base a jealous vigilance over continuity between governments. A neophyte minister naive enough to ask for background papers from a previous government will be told firmly and with punctilious courtesy that such documents may not be shared with him. The U.K. version of Hugh Heclo's account of relations between politicians and career bureaucrats in the United States would take the title *Government by a Stranger*. U.K. officials, while acting as if every stone the servant, weigh in with pointed words of caution based on custodial concern for "their" department—they usually remain within only one throughout their career—and a detailed knowledge of where skeletons are buried. The fauna and flora decorating the U.K. constitutional system conceal and soften, with appeals to deep-seated beliefs, the crude and inescapable fact that permanent civil servants wield considerable political power. An examination of the relevance of similar beliefs in Canadian constitutional lore uncovers a still poorer fit with reality.

In a more substantive way, the Canadian federal constitution undermines monarchical views of sovereignty. Unlike the British Crown, the Canadian Crown speaks with eleven voices instead of one. Even if Ottawa's status as "the government" were ironclad, ministers and officials would have to contend day-in and day-out with provincial counterparts ever watchful for distortions of the sovereign will as discerned by their ministers. In fact, one provincial government—that of Quebec—openly seeks to separate itself from the rest of Canada, and it exercises extreme selectivity in judging which actions of the federal government have the rudiments of legitimacy. The result is that even federal officials who aspire to the most pristine detachment from politics find themselves engaged in hand-to-hand combat with their opposite numbers in the provinces. The euphemism for the elaborate and ever expanding complex of committees consisting of officials from both levels—federal-provincial diplomacy—understates the degree to which committee members are exposed to unvarnished exec-utive-bureaucratic politics.

The Canadian bureaucratic system has become one-party dom-inant in Ottawa. That is largely because Quebec has, through most of this century, served up such a solid block of Liberal seats that the other major party, the Progressive Conservatives (PC), rarely wins federal elections. Thus, Liberals have held the gov-ernment for over forty-two of the last fifty years. This one-party dominance eclipses any claims on the part of permanent officials that they alone must provide governmental continuity. That might be true for individual ministers, but there are too few changes of government to put the broader concept to a test.

While Liberal dominance has undermined the claim of the permanent civil service to the continuity function, it also has raised an even more profound issue: to what extent can a public service that has worked almost exclusively for one party retain its neutrality? The answer depends on your perspective. The desire of career civil servants to protect tenure, even if—"heaven for-bid"—the PCs take over, incites fervent incantations of neutrality. When Joe Clark, the PC leader, took office in 1979, he kept all but three of the Liberals' top mandarins. Yet public statements by the new Tory leader, Brian Malroney, suggested a less benign approach, as did provincial precedents in which key deputy ministers were replaced. Two successive governments in Quebec have installed large numbers of senior officials sympathetic to their party's platform, and in the past two years new governments in Manitoba and Saskatchewan also have dismissed numerous senior officials thought to have allied themselves too closely with their previous masters.

The longevity of individual prime ministers deepens concerns over the neutrality of Ottawa's senior civil service. Jack Granastein's studies of the mandarins who came into their own during the Depression and World War II reveal the hidden hand of Mackenzie King in the development of this cadre.[1] Pierre Trudeau has played an even greater role since 1968 because the unparalleled growth of government since he first became prime minister has given him an opportunity to set a new tone for the bureaucratic establishment. Trudeau presided over the changing of the guard, whereby the cerebral and cozy mandarinate of the 1950s gave way to the big-government advisers and executives of the 1970s.

More personally, Trudeau, ever looking for minds at home in his league, has not hesitated to advance relatively young officials over the heads of much more senior aspirants. The process was explained eloquently by an official in the Department of Finance when he accurately identified one of Trudeau's elect who, at the time, was still an assistant deputy minister:

> We're fortunate to have a member of the group here in Finance, [M.A.] Mickey Cohen, of course. The [prime minister] took note of his work on the resource problem, the social security review, and the Anti-Inflation Program. So, Mickey has been in contact constantly. He's unassuming, he handles [deputy ministers] superbly, he has an uncanny ability to avoid reacting before figuring out what stance he should take, he's already excelled in one career—tax law in Toronto—so he's not trying to impress anyone. In a word, he's Trudeau's type of guy. He fits in.[2]

Liberal dominance has fostered considerable collegiality between ministers and top officials. Republican administrations in the United States tend to view suspiciously the first rung of career ranks, namely office directors and branch chiefs working at the sixth level of departmental hierarchies. Progressive Conservative

1. J. L. Granastein, *The Ottawa Men: The Civil Service Mandarins, 1935–1957* (Toronto: Oxford University Press, 1982).

2. Colin Campbell and George J. Szablowski, *The Superbureaucrats: Structure and Behavior in Central Agencies* (Toronto: Macmillan, 1979), pp. 173–74.

governments in Canada would understandably become paranoid about ministers "going native" with their departments. The community of career senior officials with significant policy roles starts with the deputy minister (DM) and extends down to directors. All departments have assistant deputy ministers in between; the larger ones have assistant deputy ministers reporting through associate deputy ministers, and directors reporting through directors general.

Deputy ministers belong to the governor-in-council group, that is, they receive their appointments on the recommendation of the prime minister to the cabinet. As of September 1983, some 106 career public servants were DMs: 13 of them ranking as DM3, 26 as DM2, and 30 as DM1. However, fewer than 40 of the DMs actually served as the deputy heads of departments.[3] The others worked in extradepartmental agencies such as public corporations and regulatory commissions; indeed, 37 worked in Crown organizations not subject to the Financial Administration Act.

With the exception of eight "GXs" in associate deputy minister positions, the remaining 2,093 senior civil servants ranked as EX, with 738 graded EX1; 593, EX2; 482, EX3; 204, EX4; and 68, EX5. Normally directors do not exceed EX2, directors general, EX3, and assistant deputy ministers, EX5. By the same token, directors usually have attained at least the grade EX1, directors general EX2, and assistant deputy ministers EX3. Theoretically, rating by civil service rank rather than by positional titles allows departments greater discretion in filling vacant posts.

Recent Liberal cabinets have been long on experience; thus most ministers have worked closely at one time or another with a diverse array of career officials. Many will take especially trusted officials with them to their next department. Under these circumstances, exceptionally strong personal loyalties develop over time.

Senior Canadian officials also tend to have greater political and administrative commitments to Liberal government policies and programs because the Canadian federal government operates with a more highly structured system of cabinet committees than does the United States or the United Kingdom. Regional political imperatives dictate that various parts of the country have at least one trustee on each committee. Since there are more than thirty departments, determining which region should be represented on what specific committee is an exceedingly delicate enterprise that

3. Figures compiled by the courtesy of the Public Service Commission, External Relations Division, Ottawa, 1983.

results in overly large committees. The Committee on Economic and Regional Development, for example, has twenty members. Ministers often find it difficult to keep up with their committee obligations. To cite an extreme case, a former finance minister, who also served as a deputy prime minister, belonged to nine of the cabinet's thirteen standing committees.

Ministers must frequently deputize officials to represent them when scheduling conflicts preclude personal coverage of meetings. In the United States and the United Kingdom, on the other hand, career officials usually do not fill in for principals simply to assure departmental representation. However, the uniqueness of the Canadian practice does not end here. Canadian ministers normally bring career officials with them when they personally cover committee meetings. Because they have had such access to the highest decisionmaking councils of Liberal governments, Canadian career officials have engaged much more completely than their counterparts in the United States and the United Kingdom in the executive-bureaucratic councils where key policy decisions are made. A different government trying to alter the status quo would have to reverse the course preferred by the mandarinate as well as by the party it replaced.

Administration of the senior civil service

Students of Canadian government frequently cite an old saw to highlight just how much Canada's executive-bureaucratic system has changed. From the 1930s to the 1950s, though there was a gradual growth in the number of standing committees overseeing critical policy sectors and initiatives, the mandarinate discussed and settled a great deal in informal sessions. Many of these sessions took place in the Grill Room of the Chateau Laurier Hotel in Ottawa. Although there were other dining places where they frequently met, deputy ministers in the middle part of this century tended to gather in the favored luncheon room in what was then the only elegant hotel in Ottawa. Over railroad hotel food, they would discuss their plots and differences. Doubtless the conversation would lead to who was going to fill the deputy minister post coming up in Finance or how young Robinson was doing in External. A researcher trying to discover something of the internal management procedures of higher permanent officials would hope to become a fly on the wall in the Grill Room.

Students of this early period of the Canadian mandarinate frequently make the mistake of saying that it operated much as did Whitehall's. The fact is that the Canadian variant fell considerably short of Britain's both in size and complexity: a comparison with Whitehall in the mid-nineteenth century, before the emergence of massive departments and the merit-oriented reforms championed by Trevelyan and Northcote, would be more accurate. The system ran in large part on the volunteerism of bright young academics who were interested in public service. To note a striking example, one of the period's most gifted personalities, Norman Robertson, took a junior post in the Department of External Affairs when the tiny agency could not offer him a senior assignment despite his passing the first secretary exam with flying colors.

Robertson and many of his peers shared Oxford backgrounds. Although few of the Canadians won firsts at Oxford, many had attended on Rhodes scholarships. However, nearly all succumbed to an American emphasis on professional certification after their liberal education. For the most part, they trained in economics and political science—largely in U.S. graduate schools—and then moved on to teaching posts, disproportionately at Queen's University in Kingston and at the University of Toronto. Thus, this generation of Canadian mandarins was older and better trained in specialized fields than recruits to the higher civil service in Britain. At the time, Canada's intellectual elite supplied key members of the political leadership as well as recruits into the emerging bureaucratic establishment. The two groups thus developed close ties. Indeed, several top civil servants—the case of Lester B. Pearson stands out—eventually crossed over to partisan politics.

The relative volunteerism of entrance into the Canadian mandarinate and the small size of the country's intellectual elite introduced career patterns that continue to work their effects today. More recent entrants generally have distinguished themselves outside of the government, either through advanced studies or, increasingly, through experience in the private sector. Since new officials join the public service and enter the track for senior positions mainly on the strength of their qualifications for a specific position, departments and central coordinating agencies place relatively little emphasis on in-house training for public service in comparison to their counterparts in the United Kingdom. Notwithstanding the size and complexity of the political and bureaucratic establishment in Ottawa today, both the dominance of the Liberals and the procedural features that foster collegiality between ministers and officials have produced a personalization of top appointments similar to that which the intimacy of the intellectual elite supplied from the 1930s to the 1950s.

In-house government studies have proved sharply critical of

senior personnel management.[4] They have found that officials are often ill prepared for higher posts. The blame rests with departments that have not mounted effective training programs, managers who have not assumed responsibility for training or evaluating their subordinates, and central agencies that have not provided adequate stimulus toward service-wide coordination of training and assessment.

The root of many of these problems rests with the fragmentation of responsibility for senior personnel management among three agencies. The Privy Council Office (PCO), whose career head is the clerk of the privy council and secretary to the cabinet, reports directly to the prime minister and takes the clear lead in recommending nominees to all posts rated for deputy ministers. The PCO also takes a keen interest in policy concerning senior personnel management at lower levels. The Treasury Board Secretariat—roughly the equivalent of the U.S. Office of Management and Budget—maintains statutory authority for management of the public service. This includes responsibility for allocating person-years to departments and for determining the terms and conditions of public service employment. Finally, the Public Service Commission—a quasi-independent government agency—safeguards probity and prudence in staffing, training, and appeals; it also handles, to a considerable degree, the operational sides of these functions. Efforts to coordinate these offices have proved extremely frustrating, even when the impetus for reform comes from the prime minister.

In assessing the internal administration of Canada's higher civil service, we should examine the extent to which it operates within an organizational milieu whose standards are independent of those of the political leadership. As in the United Kingdom, the top career official advising the prime minister on appointments chairs a committee of peers that reviews senior personnel policies and vets specific nominations for top vacancies. However, the Canadian body, styled the Committee on Senior Officials, has taken on an avant-garde character. Three of its four most recent chairmen were under forty-five when they assumed office, and many of its members are in the generation of relatively young deputy ministers that has risen to prominence under Trudeau. In the United Kingdom, the comparable committee still favors officials in their mid- to late fifties, and public servants rarely become deputy heads before they have turned fifty. Given the demographics of

4. Campbell and Szablowski, *The Superbureaucrats*, pp. 226–28.

the Canadian situation, the question arises as to how much the bureaucratic establishment has continued to exert internal discipline in senior personnel management. The really seasoned mandarins—those in their late fifties—have clearly yielded to a more recent generation. Did they at least impart their traditions in the process?

Recruitment and career routes

Although Canadians often assume that their higher civil service operates more like Britain's than America's, it actually does not even fall between the two systems. A close examination suggests that Canada comprises an aberrant case. As early as 1953, career data used by John Porter indicated that Canadian senior officials did not rise through stratified career routes.[5] Only one-quarter had spent their entire working lives in the public service; nearly two-thirds took on senior posts after being in the private sector. Along the same lines, P. J. Chartrand and K. L. Pond reported that in 1967 only 15 percent of senior officials had worked in government throughout their adult lives.[6] These authors also found that the officials who changed departments most frequently experienced the quickest advancement to the highest posts.

In 1977 Michael Pitfield, then clerk of the Privy Council and secretary to the cabinet, registered public alarm over the recruitment and development of senior officials. He stressed that initial entry too often was on the basis of a candidate's ability in specialized fields and that insufficient consideration was given to aptitude or skill for public service:

> The law does not provide the analytic competence necessary to evaluate programs and develop more effective alternatives. Economics teaches few political skills and little about the structure of government. Neither one nor the other provides exposure to managerial skills. . . . The business graduate came with administrative and problem-solving skills, and a smattering of economics, that made him very useful to government. What he did not have and still lacks, of course, is much of a base in goverment systems. . . . As regards value judgements, where the private sector manager makes his decision with a degree of privacy and according to a comparatively well-ordered set of values, the critical choices that face the public sector manager involve

5. John Porter, *The Vertical Mosaic: An Analysis of Social Class and Power in Canada* (University of Toronto Press, 1965), pp. 436–37.

6. P. J. Chartrand and K. L. Pond, *A Study of Executive Career Paths in the Public Service of Canada* (Chicago: Public Personnel Association, 1970), pp. 48–49.

difficult questions of accountability, of choices among competing values, and of the ethical principles that should govern unprecedented solutions.[7]

One of Pierre Trudeau's principal stated objectives when he took office in 1968 might have simply compounded the dangers that Pitfield identified in 1977. Trudeau involved himself in two efforts toward improving the creativity of the higher civil service. We have already seen the effects of his taking a personal interest in the development and assignment of officials whom he viewed as prospective deputy ministers. In addition, he set the wheels in motion for an unprecedented expansion of departments' senior complements. For instance, senior posts below the deputy-minister category increased between 11 and 26 percent from 1971 to 1975.[8] Along the way the federal government competed successfully with business corporations and universities for top talent. It did this partly by giving top officials higher salaries than were available to their opposite numbers in the United States and the United Kingdom, and partly by providing them with great responsibilities early on. All this brought compelling psychic rewards to senior officials who might otherwise have found careers elsewhere more alluring.

In the optimism of an expansionary era, Trudeau's initiatives appeared to energize the bureaucracy and make it more adaptable. In fact, they produced an unforeseen side effect that may have made matters worse than before. In a monograph titled *No Where to Go?* Nicole S. Morgan produced evidence of impending stagnation in the senior ranks.[9] Recruits who entered the public service during the Trudeau era have created a career bubble that has only begun working its way through the system. This cohort of officials, many of whom are still in their thirties, forms a disproportionately large segment of the senior ranks. Further, the majority of officials in it have risen extremely rapidly to the highest grades. As a result, a generation of public servants used to rapid promotions now faces the prospect of very little career advancement. In addition, as has happened at many universities

7. P. M. Pitfield, "Business Administration and Public Administration" (The James Gillies Alumni Lecture Series, York University, Toronto, November 23, 1977), pp. 12, 13, 16.

8. Audrey D. Doerr, *The Machinery of Government in Canada* (Toronto: Methuen, 1981).

9. Nicole S. Morgan, *No Where to Go?* (Montreal: Institute for Research in Public Policy, 1981).

with almost entirely tenured faculties, the relatively small supply of vacancies created by mandatory retirements will most certainly close off careers in the higher civil service to many capable aspirants in the next generation. In a word, stagnation might well seize the senior ranks.

To highlight the consequences of prevailing recruitment and career paths for Canadian civil servants, a recent comparison of ninety-two top personnel in Ottawa's central agencies to their counterparts in Washington and London proves instructive.[10] The Canadian senior central agents included top officials in the equivalents to Washington's White House office, Executive Office of the President, and Treasury Department. (The ninety-two Canadian respondents were, with the exception of a small number of senior officials in the prime minister's office, career civil servants.)

As compared with their counterparts in the United States and the United Kingdom, the Canadians tended to see government service as a means for advancement and more cited an interest in a specialized policy field. Furthermore, in accounting for their areas of expertise, just over half as many Canadians as Americans and Britons cited work experience in government. In defining their work goals, Canadians appeared to be less interested in giving the best possible advice to their superiors than in finding personal satisfaction by acquiring greater knowledge of how the system works or by being presented with challenging problems. As might be expected, the Canadians had considerably more than their share of "late vocations," people who opted for work in government after starting out in the private sector. Though Canadians offered the most expansive accounts of involvement in cabinet level bodies, they espoused the most traditional views of such issues as accountability and the boundary between politics and administration. The weight of such findings suggests that the relative youth, inexperience, and rapid mobility of the Canadian higher civil service has produced a generation of officials with comparatively unsophisticated views of why they entered government and how their work relates to that of other participants in the policy arena.

Education and in-service training

Though top officials in Canada have less well developed career norms than their counterparts in the United States and United Kingdom, they do possess many positive attributes. (This is not

---

10. Colin Campbell, *Governments under Stress: Political Executives and Key Bureaucrats in Washington, London, and Ottawa* (University of Toronto Press, 1983), pp. 311–15.

to deny, however, that better selection procedures and in-service training could improve the way potential senior executives are prepared for top positions.)

Today Canada's higher civil servants are recruited from a much wider base than in the 1930s and 1940s. Then most entrants received their first degrees from such elite central Canadian universities as Queen's, McGill, and the University of Toronto. Others studied at Oxford and Cambridge, a number on Rhodes scholarships. By the late 1960s, the University of Toronto still supplied the largest number of senior officials in Ottawa, but three western universities—Manitoba, British Columbia, and Alberta—had overtaken Queen's and McGill.[11] Oxford and Cambridge veterans are also much more an exception in the current generation: only four out of the ninety-two central agents interviewed in 1976 had studied at Oxford or Cambridge.[12] Many more respondents had obtained advanced degrees at either U.S. or Canadian universities. A type of educational meritocracy operates behind these figures. As teenagers, many of today's bureaucrats could not afford to attend private secondary schools or to travel far from their homes to the better colleges at the University of Toronto, Queen's, or McGill. But strong scholarship programs at top graduate schools in the United States and Canada made it easier for students who excelled in their first degree to pursue top-flight advanced programs. The federal government's need for expertise in such specialized areas as law, economics, natural sciences, engineering, and business has also contributed to the role of education in providing access to those who did not begin their studies in an elite university.[13]

Recruiting from a wider spectrum of educational institutions does more than simply break down the old-boy networks that maintained a steady flow of the nation's "best and brightest." Recruitment based on subject expertise also has accelerated the entry of socioeconomic groups previously underrepresented. A study by John Porter indicated that in 1953 most senior officials in Ottawa came from Canada's dominant social groups, including leaders in the business community.[14] Few were French Canadians, non-Anglican Protestants, or Catholics. By 1967 officials had more heterogeneous backgrounds.[15] Since then progress has con-

11. Chartrand and Pond, *Study of Executive Career Paths*, pp. 32, 34. See also Porter, *Vertical Mosaic*, pp. 425–28.

12. Campbell, *Governments under Stress*, pp. 328–31.

13. Ibid., pp. 329–30.

14. Porter, *Vertical Mosaic*, pp. 433–44.

15. Chartrand and Pond, *Study of Executive Career Paths*, pp. 32, 34.

tinued to be made. For instance, a study I did in 1976 showed that 36 percent of the central agents were Catholic, 7 percent were Jewish, 24 percent were French Canadians, and over 50 percent had fathers who had never gone to university.[16]

The relative heterogeneity of central agency officials has not made for increased responsiveness to diverse sectors of the public. Canadian officials lag behind both British and American respondents in consulting for advice and information leaders in business, unions, local governments, religious and ethnic groups, citizens groups, and academic and professional associations.[17] Only 2 percent make such contacts at least weekly; this falls sharply short of the 17 percent of U.K. respondents and the 26 percent of U.S. career officials who report such regular interaction with leaders outside government.

These findings buttress the view that little is done to promote an expansive or sophisticated view of public service among Canada's top officials. The facts present us with the paradox that the Canadians who drive the "fast lane" in the executive-bureaucratic community, when asked about accountability and interactions with outsiders, respond that federal vehicles must not exceed 55 miles per hour. We face the specter of officials unwilling to let go of the government's apron strings when the ambiguity of their work risks exposure to public input, scrutiny, and criticism.

The Canadian case presents a dilemma for reformers. On the one hand, there is evidence that poor selection and training contribute greatly to the unsophisticated orientation of Canadian officials. Aspirants for positions often get on short lists for ascriptive reasons. A provision governing political appointees to ministers' staffs, for example, allows them to apply for career positions after completing three years in the "exempt" category. Departmental screening normally consists of brief interview sessions that are nowhere near as rigorous as in Britain, where candidates attend the Civil Service Selection Board for two days and then proceed to a final interview. Canadian federal agencies have proved unequal to the task of adequately training those who show exceptional executive potential. Even the modest training facilities of the Public Service Commission have drawn such low enrollments that its staff development branch has recorded successive deficits.

On the other hand, there are equally disturbing questions about elitism. If merit-based examinations were rigidly used, would this

16. Campbell, *Governments under Stress*, p. 322.
17. Ibid., pp. 292–93.

mean that only those with high intellectual versatility would be carefully considered? If so, intense specialists would stand to lose a great deal. British-style selection boards where examiners drawn from random corners of the civil service run candidates through grueling paces to see how well they stand up under pressure would give the edge to the poised. Canada's traditional universities still produce greater numbers of that variety than the likes of York University or the University of Regina. A Canadian version of the British interview process might well bring back the times when the University of Toronto, Queen's, and McGill enjoyed special leverage in getting their graduates into government. Cabinet memoranda have suggested centralizing in-house training for the senior ranks in a National School of Public Policy and Administration along the lines of France's Ecole Nationale d'Administration (ENA). Critics, however, hasten to point up that elitism among the upper echelons of the French civil service exceeds by far that found among senior officials in Canada.

Conclusion

Students of higher civil services tend, as do many other scholars in government and politics, to look longingly across borders and oceans in the hope that somewhere in the world things work better than at home. Thus an optimism rarely found in domestic studies often raises expectations about other lands.

In comparing senior personnel management policies, Americans tend to hold the highest hopes about the domestic applicability of how things are done by Britons and vice versa. In this paper, I have appealed to these propensities by raising the Canadian case. Theoretically, Canada has borrowed from both systems. The prospect that it has combined in its management of top civil servants the best of the British and American systems probably sparked enough interest to warrant this study.

Unfortunately, there is little to suggest that Canada has put the best of the two worlds together. In fact, it might have accomplished just the opposite. Canada resolutely clings to the belief that it has a British-style career civil service structure in which all but ministers are theoretically neutral. Yet the weight of the available evidence suggests that the uppermost ranks are too strongly identified with Liberal policies and programs to serve any other party. The effects on the bureaucracy of Liberal dominance will linger long after the party's overthrow. The next party to form a government will probably have to depart from conventional practice by replacing a substantial number of deputy ministers with outsiders who have clearly compatible views of policy priorities and operational principles.

To add to the erosion of neutrality in the upper ranks, the fragmentation of responsibility for senior personnel management has undermined the internal coherence of the higher civil service. Until this problem is resolved, the recruitment and training difficulties identified in this paper will persist. Although immense institutional inertia would have to be overcome, it seems essential to concentrate responsibility for senior personnel management in just one agency. The setting of policy governing the higher civil service, the monitoring of senior personnel management by departments, and the related operational functions currently performed in three different agencies should all be performed by one. This agency should not be so closely attached to the prime minister that, assuming a significant number of appointments from outside the career service to the deputy-minister level, the entire senior cohort becomes politicized. On the other hand, the agency must not be as remote from political authority as the Public Service Commission. The Treasury Board—a cabinet committee responsible for management policy—would perhaps serve as a workable middle ground. The relevant units could either form part of the Treasury Board Secretariat or act as a separate agency reporting to the president of the Treasury Board.

In this paper, I examined the prospects for more rigorous procedures and improved facilities for recruitment and training. I believe that although the British and French approaches might not offer Canada a great deal, some adaptations might work well. A central agency responsible for senior personnel might conduct interviews—less exhaustive than those of Britain's Civil Service Selection Board—to screen applicants for specific vacancies on the basis of their aptitudes and preparedness for public service careers. Such interviews would provide a broader data base for the recruitment of entry-level professionals. Similarly, the proposed central agency could help monitor the assessment and promotion of senior personnel. Finally, it could develop a Canadian variant of France's ENA. Much of the ENA's contribution to elitism in the French civil service stems from the fact that most of its students come from only a limited number of the most prestigious secondary schools in the Paris area. Canada's recruitment system differs from France's in that people enter the senior official track later and in that they claim relatively heterogeneous backgrounds. Thus socioeconomic elitism poses much less of a threat in Canada. A college, along the lines of mid-career programs in the armed services, would run much less of a risk than the ENA of reinforcing elitist tendencies generally present in society.

The Higher Civil Service
of the Federal Republic
# of Germany

RENATE MAYNTZ

GERMAN public administration enjoys in general an image of professional competence, if not of great efficiency. Political patronage plays some role at all levels and for all ranks (possibly more in promotion than in initial recruitment), but for the tenured civil service at least, the effect of patronage is limited by rather elaborate requirements for recruitment and promotion. At the top level, of course, the issue is not so much patronage, in the sense of unequal opportunities or as a cause of administrative inefficiencies, as political legitimacy. The ideal of legislative control in modern parliamentary democracies assigns to the bureaucracy a merely instrumental role. Even in Germany, reality has never quite fitted this ideal, but for specific historical reasons, the instrumental character of the bureaucracy (and hence, the nonpartisan, professional character of the higher civil service) has remained a live issue up to the present.

The role of the higher civil service in government—whether it functions as a competent, nonpartisan, purely professional staff or plays a specifically political role, advising the executive and participating in policy development—depends not only on the characteristics of the higher civil servants themselves (their social background, professional orientation, and status as a professional group) but also on a number of contextual factors, which in the German case include the federal constitution and certain structural details of governmental organization. The constitutional distribution of power in West Germany assigns most legislative functions to the federal level, which means that policymaking is concentrated at the center. Policy implementation, on the other hand, is largely left to the German states, or *Länder*. The federal ministries, therefore, are more concerned—even in terms of working time—with developing programs than with managing them.[1]

1. Renate Mayntz and Fritz W. Scharpf, *Policymaking in the German Federal Bureaucracy* (New York: Elsevier, 1975), p. 63.

Given this fact, it is of great importance for the higher civil service that the political executive—the chancellor and his ministers—must turn to the established bureaucracy for support in fulfilling its functions.

The chancellor receives aid, information, and assistance from the civil servants in his office *(Bundeskanzleramt)*, a sizable agency of about 500 members that is organized and staffed according to the same principles as the federal ministries and that is normally headed by a state secretary. About a quarter of the agency's members are higher civil servants. In the early 1970s, an attempt was made to expand the office's traditional role of providing primarily information and advice to the chancellor and a certain measure of technical coordination to the federal ministries. The idea was to create a government-wide planning system managed by the chancellor's office. A system of planning commissioners was created; a reporting system was set up that required all ministries to supply detailed information about all major projects; and long-term planning groups were organized to spot policy-making needs based on forecasts of future developments in selected policy areas. However, these attempts to have the chancellor's office play a more active role in policymaking provoked resistance and hostility from the ministries, who felt their autonomy threatened, and the plan had to be abandoned after a relatively short time.[2]

The federal ministers, like the chancellor, turn to the bureaucracy for assistance in policy development. There is no German counterpart to the large circle of political advisers an American president typically employs. Nor is there any German counterpart to the French ministerial cabinet, which can, if one includes the numerous semiofficial *(officieux)* and unofficial *(clandestins)* members, assume quite significant proportions.[3] The leadership of a German ministry typically consists of the minister and two to four state secretaries. Aside from clerical staff, the minister and the state secretaries can each employ one personal assistant. In addition, the minister may have a press or public relations assistant and, possibly, separate assistants for cabinet and parliamentary matters. The minister's office is headed by a director who in some cases also serves as his

2. Heribert Schatz, "Auf der Suche nach Problemlösungsstrategien—Die Entwicklung der politischen Planung auf Bundesebene," in Renate Mayntz and Fritz W. Scharpf, eds., *Planungsorganisation* (Munich: Piper and Co., 1973); and Klaus Seemann, *Entzaubertes Bundeskanzleramt* (Landshut: Verlag Politisches Archiv, 1975).

3. Frido Wagener and Bernd Rückwardt, *Führungshilfskräfte in Ministerien* (Baden-Baden: Nomos, 1982), p. 56.

personal assistant; the director is not usually the formal superior of the entire personal staff, since some or all of the specialized assistants have direct access to the minister. The small size of this staff is significant; so is the fact that the overwhelming majority of staff members are career civil servants. Of the sixty-eight personal assistants and directors in one minister's office in 1980, only six were not civil servants.[4]

Given these structural features and the fact that the political executive (not parliament) plays the dominant role in policy development, policymaking in Germany is and indeed must be the responsibility of higher civil servants in the federal bureaucracy.

Features of the career service

In West Germany there is no special civil service department to oversee the day-to-day management of the service or to look after its special interests. The responsibility for general questions relating to the civil service, including annual salary adjustments or changes in civil service law, rests with the Ministry of the Interior; day-to-day management issues are left to the ministries. This does not create friction nor endanger the uniformity of the service because the structure of the German civil service is clear-cut and not overly complex. Moreover, there is a rather elaborate and uniform (that is, service-wide) set of rules that guides training, recruitment, and personnel management in the service. A special civil service department is not necessary.

The German civil service includes employees as well as tenured officials. Most higher civil servants in the federal bureaucracy are tenured; only a small number in top positions are outsiders or lateral entrants. If the members of this minority group fulfill the educational requirements of the higher civil service, they can—and very often do—become tenured officials, even though this requires special procedures including further training and an okay by the Federal Personnel Committee.

Tenured civil servants are usually recruited for a career, that is, for entry into a category and not for a specific position. Most officials in the federal ministries belong to the so-called general administrative service, a functional category that plays a generalist kind of role. Most higher officials in this service have trained in law, a field of study that seems to provide civil servants with a considerably better chance to reach top positions.[5] Thus, roughly

4. Ibid, p. 28.
5. Niklas Luhmann and Renate Mayntz, *Personal im öffentlichen Dienst: Eintritt und Karrieren* (Baden-Baden: Nomos 1973), p. 142.

two-thirds of those who occupy top positions in the federal bureaucracy are jurists.

Though it is no longer correct to speak of a "monopoly of jurists," the predominance of legally trained higher civil servants remains a subject of heated debate. On the one hand, it is argued that long-range public planning and policymaking call for substantive expertise, which jurists rarely receive in the course of their academic careers. (Their training is strictly in *law*, particularly private law.) On the other hand, however, the legalistic bent of the German political culture, which finds prominent expression in the principle of administration by law, puts a premium on the ability to give policy decisions the proper legal form. In fact, most policy work in the federal ministries consists of drafting laws, decrees, and ordinances. For this reason legally trained higher officials in the general administrative service are not considered legal specialists but generalists able to fill a wide variety of positions. (This views accords with our mobility data about these officials.)

The German system of higher education does not operate with competitive entrance examinations (like the French *concours*), and it confers general qualifications which may or may not be related to the specific needs (or availability) of given positions.[6] This observation also holds for the training and recruitment of civil servants. To bridge the gap, prospective higher civil servants, having received their first academic degree (a rough equivalent of a good American M.A.), must enlist in a special preparatory service that provides both theoretical and on-the-job training.

Law students enter this preparatory service after their first legal examinations. Even for them, the training is not specifically related to an administrative career; rather it provides the law students with practical experience in public administration and in the work of a lawyer and of the courts. Accordingly, law students may choose more wisely among these careers when they conclude the preparatory service with their second legal examinations.

Students with a nonlegal academic background (economists or social scientists) who wish to enter either the general administrative service, the technical service, or some other specialized service (engineering, medicine, agricultural economics) also pass through a preparatory phase, but in these cases the training is specifically aimed at familiarizing them with the administrative context in which they later will have to work.

6. Helmut Coing, *Ausbildung von Elitebeamten in Frankreich und Grossbritannien* (Berlin: Duncker & Humblot, 1983), p. 50.

This combined system of academic education and special training is supplemented by a number of institutions that provide specialized further education. One of these is the School of Administrative Sciences (Hochschule für Verwaltungswissenschaften) in Speyer, a postgraduate school that provides a small group of future officials (mainly recruits to the general administrative service who have a previous education in law) with a specialized preparation in administrative science. The Hochschule had once been expected to become a kind of German Ecole Nationale d'Administration, but its real role has remained much more modest.

The other specialized institutions are in-service training academies catering to the personnel of specific ministries (Defense, Foreign Service, Finance, Railroad and Post, Telephone and Telegraph), or to the general administrative service class. The latter institution, the Federal Academy for Public Administration (Bundesakademie für öffentliche Verwaltung), offers about eighty courses annually to higher civil servants in the federal bureaucracy. Most of the courses last a week or less, and they are attended by 1,500 to 1,700 people, or more than 10 percent of the respective target group each year. Some courses are introductory in nature, providing legal training to nonjurists and training in economics, planning, decision theory, and organization to jurists. Nearly half the courses deal with various aspects of personnel management and leadership. By and large, the academy provides job-related education to generalists rather than advanced, specialized training to experts.

Recruitment and promotional decisions are departmental prerogatives. Only one agency has government-wide functions in the field of personnel management, the Federal Personnel Committee (*Bundespersonalausschuß*). It is a small committee whose functions are primarily consultative. It is involved in recruitment decisions only in those exceptional cases in which candidates do not possess the normal career prerequisites and in promotional decisions only when these involve exceptions from the formal rules.

Within the federal departments, personnel management is handled by a specialized section in the general service division. Promotion is based on seniority, with performance as a secondary criterion. To aid promotional decisions, civil servants are subject to a periodic written evaluation by their immediate superior. In the case of top positions, from section chief upward, the state secretary or even the minister himself is directly involved in making personnel decisions, which at these ranks also need formal cabinet approval: the chancellor's autonomous power of appointment is restricted to ministers only. The power of self-administration, which holds for the vast majority of personnel decisions in the civil service, does not apply to the most influential positions in the bureaucracy.

It may not come as a surprise, but is still worth noting, that the career lines of politicians and civil servants, especially tenured officials, are quite distinct. The lines become blurred only at the level of the state secretaries. Normally a career in the higher civil service does not lead to a high political office. Ministers, on the other hand, are clearly politicians, even though some of them may have worked in public administration before starting their political careers.[7] If a civil servant aspires to be a minister, therefore, he would do better to renounce his bureaucratic career and become a professional politician.

Formal training requirements and the principles governing recruitment and promotion are largely responsible for career lines remaining distinct. According to the principles of the German civil service, tenured officials are normally recruited at the lowest of the five ranks within a given category since, in principle, the four higher ranks are filled through promotion. Direct recruitment of outsiders to higher positions violates this rule and is resented by career staffers who see their chances for promotion impaired. Though the personal rank and pay of an official is not fully determined by the position he occupies, there is a significant correlation between personal rank and position. It is against this background that the actual influx of outsiders must be evaluated.

Advancement in personal rank and pay is the most frequent type of mobility among German civil servants. The frequency of promotions, especially those involving a positional change, is primarily a function of length of service and of certain structural factors that determine the availability of openings.[8] There is also a substantial amount of horizontal mobility, especially between different task areas. Higher civil servants in the federal ministries, especially those working in the general administrative service, are the most mobile group in the German bureaucracy.[9]

7. Rolf-Peter Lange, "Auslesestrukturen bei der Besetzung von Regierungsämtern," in J. Dittberner and R. Ebbighausen, eds., *Parteiensysteme in der Legitimationskrise* (Opladen: Westdeutscher Verlag, 1973), pp. 165, 143. For more details, see Renate Mayntz, "German Federal Bureaucrats: A Functional Elite between Politics and Administration," in E. Suleiman, ed., *Higher Civil Servants in the Policymaking Process: A Comparative Exploration* (New York: Holmes and Meier, 1983).

8. Luhmann and Mayntz, *Personal im öffentlichen Dienst*, p. 173.

9. Ibid., pp. 183, 189.

While most of this mobility is intra-ministerial, the degree of similarity among the task areas within one ministry should not be overestimated. For instance, in the course of a career at the Ministry of the Interior, an official may work in such diverse fields as foreign immigration, environmental protection, civil service reform, and the observation of terrorist movements. Task continuity is often higher among those who do not reach top positions since a change in task area is often the price of a promotion. If one accepts self-identification as a specialist as a valid indicator, the degree of specialization within the German civil service is lowest among top office holders in the general administrative service at the federal level.

The combined effect of these tendencies is that only a minority of top federal bureaucrats consider themselves to be specialists rather than generalists.[10]

Politicization in the higher civil service

The German political executive, no less than his counterparts elsewhere, wants and needs collaborators who are not only loyal in the sense of fulfilling given orders but also committed to the executive's political outlook and program. Lacking a sufficiently large and freely disposable personal staff and forced to rely mainly on civil servants for help, the German political executive would be faced with a very serious problem were it not for two institutions specifically designed to bridge the gap between politics and administration. One of these, the parliamentary state secretary (*parlamentarischer Staatssekretär*), is of fairly recent origin, while the other, a category of civil servants known as political officials (*politische Beamte*), has a venerable tradition.

The office of parliamentary state secretary (PStS) was created in 1967. The PStS must be a member of parliament and his term of office ends with the legislative period. He serves as a deputy to his minister in cabinet meetings and especially in parliament, where he may answer questions addressed to the department during question time, respond to formal parliamentary requests for information, and even take part in plenary debates.[11] The parliamentary state secretary has to maintain close contact with various party groups to which he, being a member of a political party himself, has better access than would be true for most career civil servants. The PStS shares in departmental management, but here too his function is political rather than managerial. In the beginning, only the larger federal ministries designated a PStS; today several of them have two, so that there are now twenty

10. Ibid., p. 205.

11. Rainer Wahl, "Die Weiterentwicklung der Institution des parlamentarischen Staatssekretärs," *Der Staat,* vol. 8 (1969), p. 334.

parliamentary state secretaries in the German government.[12] Most of the seventy-six men who have served since 1976 were simply members of parliament. A few, however, had already served a term as a PStS or had even been a minister. Only in some exceptional cases did a former (tenured) state secretary, having entered the realm of politics, become a PStS later on.

Parliamentary state secretaries are, in terms of background and function, a distinctly political group. This is less true of the much larger group of political officials, a special category of civil servants who can be temporarily retired at any time, the rationale being that they hold positions in which full agreement with the goals of a given government is essential. This category is clearly defined by law, mainly the Federal Civil Service Law of 1953. The institution as such, however, is not an invention of the Federal Republic of Germany; the need to legally dispose of civil servants in top positions for political reasons made itself felt almost as soon as there was a tenured civil service. The institution was given roughly its present shape 130 years ago.

Political officials are circumscribed in different ways at the various levels of the political system. At the federal level, political officials hold the ranks of state secretary and division chief (*Ministerialdirektor*). There are also a relatively large number of political officials in the Foreign Service and in certain special positions like chief of the Press Office. Political officials are not appointed as such. They are mainly career civil servants who move into this category by being promoted to the corresponding ranks. This means that normal civil service criteria apply, in principle at least, to the selection and appointment of political officials. The ease with which they can be disposed of, on the other hand, stands in sharp contrast to the job protection enjoyed by other tenured civil servants. If a political official is sent into temporary retirement, the minister need not give any reasons for his decision; the official is paid the pension he is entitled to according to his rank and age.[13]

Political officials make it easier for the political executive to bring the bureaucracy into line, to make sure that those who develop policies do so in agreement with the intentions of the party in power *without* needing explicit instructions. As desirable as this may be for the political executive, it raises the question of

12. Hans-Ulrich Derlien, "Fluktuation politischer Beamter in der Ministerialverwaltung des Bundes" (1983), pp. 50ff.

13. Dieter Kugele, *Der politische Beamte: Eine Studie über Genesis, Motiv, Bewährung und Reform einer politisch-administrativen Institution* (Munich: Tuduv, 1976).

whether the civil service can be politicized and to what degree this will impair its professional competence. I will touch on three aspects of this question: the extent to which political considerations determine top-level personnel decisions, especially in connection with a change in government; the extent to which the institution of political officials opens the civil service to outsiders; and the changes in orientation of top officials that follow from this.

To begin with, it is important to realize the rather small size of the group under review here. The core group of political officials (excluding the lower levels in the Foreign Office) consists of 24 tenured state secretaries and 110 officials with the ranks B9/B10, mostly division chiefs.[14] Counting all top positions down to the level of section chief, the total is about 1,700 positions: the German federal bureaucracy is a rather steep pyramid.

In the normal run of a legislative period, the majority of political officials who leave the service retire because they have reached the age limit. Others ask for premature retirement for reasons of ill health. Only a minority (about 10 percent) are sent into temporary retirement by their ministers.[15] But this changes dramatically at the time of a change in government, especially if this involves a change in the governing majority. If one takes the most recent change of government (1982–83) as an example, forty-four political officials temporarily retired (half of the tenured state secretaries and less than a third of the division chiefs). These retirements included several persons that either did not belong to any party or belonged to the smaller coalition party. Sometimes a change in government and the chance to retire officeholders for apparently political reasons affords the opportunity to get rid of an incompetent official without causing him to lose face. At any rate, these figures show that the existing legal chances of reassignment were only partly used.

However, the politically induced amount of fluctuation is greater than the number of temporary retirements indicates. With the recent change to a government dominated by the Christian Democrats and Christian Socialists, about 40 top officials (most of them below the level of division chief and hence not in the category of political officials) who were either members or known sympathizers of the Social Democratic party were transferred to other positions, nearly always of less importance. In addition, most of the personal staff of ministers and state secretaries was changed, including the clerical staff and, in at least one known

14. Derlien, "Fluktuation politischer Beamter."
15. Ibid.

case, even the driver of the ministerial limousine. This amounted to an additional 200 people, of whom about 90 were higher civil servants.[16] Leaving these 200 people out of consideration, but taking into account that a number of new divisions and sections were created by the new government, a total of about 100 top-level line positions were available to be filled with new incumbents.

To illustrate what this means for a given ministry, let us take as an example the Ministry of the Interior. As of April 1983, four division chiefs had been sent into temporary retirement and one advanced to state secretary in another ministry; the remaining six retained their positions. The five vacancies at this level were filled with four internal and one external recruit (the former police chief of Munich). In addition, the two parliamentary state secretaries and their personal assistants—as well as all of the important members in the minister's personal staff—were changed, the newcomers again coming mainly from within the ministry, while the outgoing personnel were transferred to other positions without leaving the department. Though all this meant quite some re-shuffling, especially if the second-order movements induced by the primary transferrals are counted in, it is obvious that the personal costs for most of the civil servants involved were modest.

What is even more striking in this example is the fact that most of the newcomers were recruited from within the federal civil service and even from within the same ministry. The same thing holds for those reassigned to other ministries: there are new faces behind a number of desks, but the faces are mainly familiar ones.

Despite the charges of some critics, it is difficult to establish conclusively that the wave of reassignments that took place with the 1982–83 change of government was much higher than that which occurred with the advent of the Social Democratic–Liberal coalition in 1969. In 1969 we had the classical case of a new "leftist" government faced with a presumably conservative bureaucracy that had been strengthened in its inclinations by a succession of conservative governments. After thirteen years of government dominated by the Social Democrats, a substantial number of reassignments was only to be expected. In fact, one attempted comparison suggested that there was no significant difference between the number of reassignments now and then.[17] What may be significantly different, however, is the extent to which vacancies were filled by outsiders. While some observers

16. The figures come from a personal communication and are based on a semiofficial compilation as of May 1983.

17. Derlien, "Fluktuation politischer Beamter."

noted that "leftist" federal administrators were typically brought in as lateral entrants to the bureaucracy after 1969, the new "conservative" government, though fully using its legal powers to select key officials it trusted, did not seem to feel constrained to look for such persons outside the federal bureaucracy.[18]

In Germany most high-level vacancies continue to be filled by career civil servants even though it is understood that political criteria can play a legitimate role in recruiting outsiders to high positions in the federal bureaucracy. During the early 1970s, the last period for which such data are available, only one out of every four political officials was an outsider, that is, a lateral entrant to the federal bureaucracy. The proportion of outsiders in positions just below the top ranks was even smaller.[19] This shows that while the institution of political officials does facilitate the entry of outsiders, countervailing pressures—formal entry requirements and the general expectation that higher positions will be filled by promotion from below—put rather effective constraints on this mechanism. In contrast to Heclo's description of the American case, this is no "government of strangers."

Obviously political criteria can also be used in filling top positions from within the service. The percentage of outsiders is, therefore, not a valid indicator for the effective politicization of the higher civil service. Nevertheless, the recruitment of outsiders serves to increase the proportion of political party members in the service; in the early 1970s, over two-thirds of the outsiders, but only one-fourth of career civil servants in top positions, belonged to a party.[20] In general, party membership increases sharply with rank: while the vast majority of state secretaries are party members, this proportion drops to about half and then again to about a third at the next two lower levels. To a large extent, this distribution is the effect of selective promotion by political criteria. Perception of such a selective tendency could well increase the readiness of ambitious civil servants to join a party early in their career, but this is a sword that cuts two ways, since joining the "wrong" party may be as detrimental to quick advancement as being a member of the "right" one may help.

As for the orientation of top German bureaucrats, it is obvious that the recruitment practices described have had their effects.

18. Joel D. Aberbach, Robert D. Putnam, and Bert A. Rockman, *Bureaucrats and Politicians in Western Democracies* (Harvard University Press, 1981), p. 167.

19. Hans-Günther Steinkemper, *Amtsträger im Grenzbereich zwischen Regierung und Verwaltung* (Frankfurt/Main: P. D. Lang, 1980), pp. 108ff.

20. Ibid., p. 124.

Empirical studies of the attitudes of higher civil servants show that the idealized stereotype of the Weberian (or the nineteenth century Prussian) official does not fit today's reality.[21] Robert Putnam characterized the predominant orientation of today's top-level federal officials quite well when he described the "political bureaucrat" in contrast to his "classical" counterpart. The political bureaucrat, Putnam says, is

> both more aware of "political realities" and more willing to treat political influences on policymaking as legitimate. He recognizes the need to bargain and compromise, yet at the same time he does not necessarily shrink from advocating and even fighting for his own preferred policies. Whereas the classical bureaucrat is "procedure-oriented" or "rule-oriented," the political bureaucrat is "problem-oriented" or "program-oriented." Whereas the classical bureaucrat views the politician as a troublesome or even dangerous antagonist, interfering with the efficiency and objectivity of government, the political bureaucrat sees the politician instead as a participant in a common game, one whose skills and immediate concerns may differ from his own, but whose ultimate values and objectives are similar.[22]

One should not construct too close and simple a linkage between attitudinal change and the growing importance of party membership and party allegiance for recruitment to top bureaucratic positions. For one thing, top civil servants in Germany have never been an apolitical group, nor has political abstinence been a normative expectation. All that the civil service law of today requires is that officials fulfill their tasks in a nonpartisan way and observe such moderation and self-restraint in their political activities as seems necessary in view of their position and official function. Judging from court sentences, only extremely radical deviations from what might be called political moderation are considered as violations of this norm.[23]

Second, there is a general process of attitudinal change at work. It is a generational phenomenon and holds for the entire civil service; it amounts to a shift away from the functional self-image as "servant of the state" to that of an "advocate of the public," an inherently more partisan role.[24] The ascendance of the "political

21. Peter Grottian, "Zum Planungsbewusstsein der Bonner Ministerialorganisation," *Politische Vierteljahresschrift,* Sonderheft 4 (1972); and Robert D. Putnam, "The Political Attitudes of Senior Civil Servants in Britain, Germany, and Italy," in Mattei Dogan, ed., *The Mandarins of Western Europe: The Political Role of Top Civil Servants* (Wiley, 1975).

22. Putnam, "Political Attitudes," p. 90.

23. Jochen Frowein, *Die politische Bestätigung des Beamten* (Tübingen: Mohr/Siebeck, 1976).

24. Luhmann and Mayntz, *Personal im öffentlichen Dienst.*

bureaucrat" is therefore part of a much wider process of change that, aside from reflecting generational experience, accords very well with the actual functions to be performed by the different levels within the administrative system.

Even so, German higher civil servants in the federal bureaucracy are not yet examples of the "pure hybrid," that fusion of bureaucrat and politician identified by Aberbach, Putnam, and Rockman as the role image of the future,[25] which, for a number of structural reasons, seems to be approximated more by the United States than by any of the European countries studied at this seminar. In Germany only a small minority of high federal officials are sufficiently politicized to be called "bureaucratic politicians" rather than "political bureaucrats." The vast majority displays a general orientation clearly different from that of politicians: while bureaucrats are political in the sense of being policy-oriented (or program-oriented, in Putnam's language), politicians are political in the sense of a dominant power orientation. As a result, the relationship between politicians and bureaucrats is not without conflict. Both sides are often irritated by the other's apparent intransigence: the politician's refusal to "listen to reason" (that is, the bureaucrat's expert opinion) grates on the civil servant while the latter's insistence on what is impracticable annoys the politician. In spite of relatively frequent contacts with politicians, especially members of the Bundestag, and the relative frequency of party membership among top officials, open attempts by politicians to interfere directly in the day-to-day operations of a ministry, including the development of policy proposals, tend to be strongly resisted.

An evaluation   What is the effect of all of this on the quality and performance of the German higher civil service? A valid answer to the question presupposes standards of objective measurement, or at least a comparison with other systems or periods, in order to arrive at some rank ordering. Neither is available for this analysis, so the following tentative conclusions serve to highlight certain aspects of the German case rather than evaluate it in any strict sense.

1   Top civil servants play an important role in policymaking, they enjoy power and influence in their own right and do not simply function as temporary aides to the political executive. On the positive side, this provides a continuity not found in other forms of an advisory staff. On the negative side, this very

25. *Bureaucrats and Politicians,* p. 17.

continuity contributes to the power of the civil service, which is not without danger.

2. German political executives entering office find a reservoir of experienced civil servants from which they can choose their lieutenants. On the one hand, this is clearly positive and potentially contributes to the quality of policy development. On the other hand, this also means that political executives are restricted in the choice of their close collaborators; they find it very difficult to bring in people who lack the formal educational prerequisites or to recruit short-term assistance (as for a task force).

3. Since the people who take over personal staff and top line-positions after a change in government are not outsiders, but are recruited from within the civil service, such reassignments do not basically disrupt the continuity of the bureaucracy. But this phenomenon also has both positive and potentially negative implications.

4. German higher civil servants are basically well trained, but the dominant type of training makes most of them better able to fulfill generalist roles in a line capacity than to perform specialized jobs. While the general level of competence is therefore relatively high, it remains doubtful whether top civil servants are optimally prepared for the job of policy development.

5. The restricted "catchment area" and the generally small size of the expert staff in the ministries limit the planning capacity of the government; moreover, the character of this staff and its subjection to the organizational and personnel management norms of the civil service make adjustments to new tasks difficult.

6. Though both bureaucrats and politicians are involved in policy development, the persisting difference in role conception and outlook maintains a functional differentiation that might well be superior to a virtual fusion of these roles.

The Higher Civil Service of France

BERNARD GOURNAY

AN AMERICAN professor once noted that "the political role played by top civil servants in Britain is complex, subtle and often misunderstood."[1] He could well have said the same about highly placed French civil servants. Thus it is difficult to summarize, in the space of a few pages, a system that is necessarily very complicated. A mixture of the old and the new, of unity and fragmentation, of legal rules and extralegal practices, French institutions cannot be described with a few simple ideas. The political-governmental elites in France oversee a machine of vast proportions: a state machinery that employs almost as many people as the U.S. federal government, a very large nationalized sector, and social welfare institutions closely controlled by different ministries.

Administrators and politicians

Four distinct groups can be identified in the upper reaches of the French government: first, the members of the government, including the president, the prime minister, and 20 to 30 ministers who are aided by 10 to 20 deputy ministers (*secrétaires d'état*); second, the members of the ministerial cabinets, some 500 to 700 executives who are temporarily appointed to aid the members of the government (30 to 40 for the president, 50 to 70 for the prime minister, 10 to 20 for each minister, and 5 to 10 for each deputy minister); third, directors, including 100 to 150 department directors and 150 to 200 heads of public establishments; and fourth, career higher civil servants, who work either under the authority of the ministers (3,000 to 5,000), or in a relatively independent fashion in corps or inspection offices (600 to 700).

The responsibilities of the groups mentioned above are in theory similar to those of their counterparts in other countries. In practice, however, the role of the directors, and particularly of the depart-

1. James B. Christoph, "High Civil Servants and the Politics of Consensualism in Great Britain," in Mattei Dogan, ed., *The Mandarins of Western Europe: The Political Role of Top Civil Servants* (Wiley, 1975), p. 25.

ment directors (*directeurs ministeriels*), is variable and often ambiguous. They are charged with at least three tasks: to furnish the ministers with information on all questions within their jurisdiction; to implement the decisions made by the political leaders; and to supervise the daily functioning of the units under them and handle any difficulties that might arise.

Not all directors participate equally in political decisionmaking. Department directors, as governmental counselors, are in competition not only with the members of the ministerial cabinets but also with the general staffs of the president and the prime minister.[2] It is generally believed that the role and the influence of department directors has diminished since the beginning of the Fifth Republic.

In the French system there are many higher civil servants and former career civil servants in the upper spheres of the political-administrative system. Most upper executive positions are, in fact, occupied by career administrators. This is also true of the ministerial cabinets and the advisers to the prime minister and the president. Ever since the beginning of the Fifth Republic, the French government itself has been composed of a large number of former career administrators.

What kind of rapport exists between political authorities and the civil service in a country where there is no clear doctrine or set of rules to define the respective roles of the groups involved? Numerous books and articles have been written about the relationships among ministers, their deputies, ministerial cabinets, and career administrators.[3] These often lively critiques have examined the behavior of each of the four groups mentioned above; many have focused in particular on members of the ministerial cabinets, who are accused of being the biggest problem.

Conflicts do arise between politicians and career administrators, sometimes about the content of decisions, but more often about the functional role each plays in the governmental and administrative systems. The ministers, often with reason, defy higher civil servants who want to impose their views on their superiors, even though in France—and here our traditions differ from those of Great Britain—administrators are expected to play an active role in the life of the nation. As for civil servants, they sometimes consider their ministers to be incompetent amateurs, more con-

2. Ezra N. Suleiman, *Politics, Power, and Bureaucracy in France: The Administrative Elite* (Princeton University Press, 1974).

3. There is a fairly complete bibliography in ibid. See also *Les Superstructures des Administrations Centrales* (Paris: Institut Français des Sciences Administratives, 1973).

cerned with their personal careers and politics than with their present jobs.

These conflicts, which often could be resolved by frank face-to-face discussions, often smoulder because no one talks to anyone else. There are a large number of higher civil servants who complain about never being able to meet with their ministers to discuss seriously the problems that they both face. These tensions, described by Suleiman and others, are at the root of many difficulties, delays, and blockages that plague French administration, particularly in certain cabinet positions.[4]

Still, I believe that the consequences of such conflicts are not as dramatic as one might believe at first. Generally speaking, the French—and higher civil servants are no exception—have a strong penchant for polemic discussion; they aggressively assert their personalities and their attitudes by denouncing, in abstract terms, the behavior of the "others," that is, the groups of which they are not a part.

In daily life, however, their actions are much more measured and are generally marked by great prudence. Ministers, members of ministerial cabinets, directors, and career civil servants usually manage to cooperate in an acceptable manner. The governmental-administrative system often functions with an exasperating inertia, which does not preclude fits of feverish and hectic movement. Projects that are abandoned or not even begun, or that deviate from their original goals, are numerous. However, this does not prevent the political machine from functioning: laws are voted on; budgets are adopted; programs are executed (at least in part). If one examines the overall achievements of the French state over the past twenty-five years, it is impossible to be completely satisfied; still nothing justifies the verbal pessimism that is so widespread in France.

It seems to me that relations between political authorities and the higher civil service in France are neither very good nor very bad; things operate with an average efficacy similar to that in other European countries of comparable size. This relative efficiency is explained, in part, by one fact: ministers, members of the ministerial cabinets, department directors, and career administrators frequently have a common origin: the public service.

4. Suleiman, *Politics, Power, and Bureaucracy*. Guy Thuillier, a high civil servant and an acute observer of the political-administrative scene in France, says such tensions may result not only in misunderstandings and quarrels but also in the deliberate retention of information, political maneuvering, and intrigues. See Guy Thuillier, *Les Cabinets Ministeriels* (Paris: Presses Universitaires de France, 1982).

*Governing
the higher
civil service*

French practice is a compromise between a system in which the higher civil service is completely in the hands of the political authorities and one in which career administrators are entirely self-governing. The French government has at its command the power to appoint, to displace, and to dismiss the most important of the higher civil servants. But its power is not absolute; it must respect certain norms and traditions.

Article 13 of the French constitution enumerates the posts whose holders are designated to the council of ministers.[5] These nominations are, in principle, discretionary: the government can choose whomever it wants, even if the candidate is not a part of the higher civil service. (The same is true for other positions enumerated by the decrees that complete the list in the constitution: the chiefs of the great public establishments and the principal leaders of national enterprises.) The total number of discretionary positions is about 400.

The French government makes wide use of its nominating powers. Since the beginning of the Fifth Republic, it has appointed to these key positions men who have not had the usual profile. The socialist government that took power in May 1981 has gone even further, nominating for many high national positions men who have never been a part of the higher civil service: union officials, journalists, politicians, and even a man who came straight from the private sector.

How are these appointments made? Cabinet ministers propose candidates acceptable to the prime minister and the president. Thus members of the ministerial cabinets may be called on to act as department directors, to head public establishments, or to run public enterprises. Often enough, though, the president or the prime minister imposes on some department his own candidate (whether or not the person so chosen is part of its circle).

The politicians' margin of choice is limited, however, by some unwritten laws, which are respected in nine out of ten cases. The most notable of these is that the person selected must come from the higher civil service, and more specifically, from the category of higher civil servants designated "A." By law these administrators are recruited through an examination equivalent to that of the National School of Administration (Ecole Nationale d'Admin-

5. These positions include department directors of the central administration, ministerial directors, school rectors (responsible for regional educational services), government representatives in the overseas departments, ambassadors, and military generals. Counselors in the Council of State and advisers to the Auditor's Agency are normally designated without intervention from the political authority.

istration, or ENA) and the *grandes écoles*. This rule limits the number of individuals eligible for appointment. There are also other norms that further reduce the politicians' freedom of choice by reserving the directorships of certain departments for a category (or a small number of categories) of higher civil servants. It is impossible to describe these norms in just a few lines because they vary from one post to another. Suffice it to say that the criteria for exclusion are all the more strict since the departments are powerful and the bodies from which the selected habitually are chosen are very prestigious. Thus, in the Department of Economy and Finance—one of the stronger departments—the central administration directorships are never occupied by anyone who is not a part of the club. These posts are, in fact, reserved for financial inspectors and civil administrators; the balance between the two groups is held in a subtle equilibrium. In the same vein, the corps of higher civil servants who come from the *grandes écoles* monopolize the majority of managerial positions in certain ministries, such as Industry and Transportation, and in the establishments that depend on them. In the less solid or less prestigious departments (Labor, Health, Culture, and so on), political authorities have a greater freedom of choice: they can designate men who are members of the department or they can call on outsiders without provoking any difficulties.[6]

The government does more than designate and dismiss higher civil servants. It also makes decisions that reach further down within the civil service. Thus cabinet ministers and directors can influence nominations to positions below the director level and also to positions in field services. It is not easy to appreciate the importance of these influences, but they are real. Political sympathies can play a certain role, but the majority of higher civil servants in France do not belong to a political party. Personal contacts, friendships, and departmental loyalties explain a greater number of the choices made.

Another means for French political authorities to influence the careers of certain higher civil servants is the *tour extérieur,* or "nomination around the periphery," by which civil servants are transferred from one administrative body to another. In the Council of State (*Conseil d'Etat*), the Auditor's Agency (*Cordes*

6. Higher civil servants who are deprived of their posts do not cease to belong to the civil service and can continue to follow their careers. Those who come from juridical bodies like the Council of State or the Auditor's Agency, from large technical bodies like the Bureau of Mines or the Bureau of Bridges and Roads, or from the university may retake their old positions and ultimately attain higher posts with greater responsibilities.

Comptes), the Inspectorate General of Finance, and many other inspectorates, ministers can appoint to certain positions the higher civil servants of their choice. In such nominations, friendships and personal contacts, as well as political convictions, play a real (though variable) role.

The preceding discussion has shown the ways in which politicians may make decisions that affect the careers of higher civil servants. I would now like to stress, in more general terms, the institutions and practices of self-administration that give French higher civil servants a fairly high degree of autonomy.

Self-administration is practiced on two levels. On the first is a system of rules (written and unwritten) that apply to the entire higher civil service; these rules are to a large extent made and maintained by central agencies like the Council of State. On the second level are rules peculiar to the departments and to the corps of higher civil servants. Through its powers of self-administration, the French higher civil service can compel the government to take account of its wishes.

The general principles that govern the higher civil service are found in the General Statute of the Civil Service and in the customs that have been developed therefrom. It is not necessary to list here all of these rules. One need merely recall the most important of them. The first deals with the conditions for entrance into an administrative position: a passing grade on the competitive written examinations that are intended to ensure that everyone begins with an equal chance for success; proof of high intelligence; approval by independent juries composed largely or entirely of higher civil servants; and in-service training by the various ministries. The second set of rules governs the guarantees given to higher civil servants in the development of their careers; state agents have a right to advancement based in large part on seniority. Finally, the French higher civil service enjoys total employment security; they have the right to "stay for life" within the administration.

Three units watch over the French higher civil service. The Council of State ensures that the general rules described above are kept. It does this in three ways: by recommendations—usually followed—that it gives to the government concerning legislative and regulatory texts relative to the rights of the higher civil service; by the judgments it renders on individual appeals; and by the great authority it enjoys within the administration and, more generally, within French society.

The Office of the General Director of Administration and the

Civil Service is in principle the central personnel agency of the government; it is supposed to counsel the government on and watch over the implementation of decisions concerning the higher civil service. Since its creation in 1945, however, its role has been relatively limited. Its principal activity has been to manage the interministerial corps of civil administrators; by no means is it meant to evaluate the professional quality of higher civil servants.

The Budget Office, attached to the Department of Economy and Finance, is the third central office charged with personnel issues: it concerns itself with remunerating all higher civil servants, a power that is uncontestable but essentially negative. The office has neither the ambition nor the means to conceive of and apply wider policies governing higher civil servants.

Thus the three central units charged with running the higher civil service system in France ensure the maintenance of the system but do not really govern it. This is left to departmental personnel offices and the managerial staffs of the *grands corps*. They endeavor, in as many ways as possible, to improve the quality of recruitment and to respond to the needs of French civil servants. They try not only to maintain but also to improve the advantages and benefits for the people for whom they have responsibility. Thus the corps of higher civil servants in France has some veritable powers that the government must recognize. Ministers can modify the laws that regulate the corps, and they have made certain reforms since the beginning of the Fifth Republic, but this requires a lot of energy.

The compensation system for the higher civil service is neither logical nor clear. To a large extent, it is unfair. Top administrators receive set salaries determined by the official scale as well as bonuses and other remunerations, which may range from 5 percent to 100 percent of the base salary. The most favored state officials are administrators in the Department of Economy and Finance and some categories of engineers. The civil servants who occupy high posts in the many publicly owned concerns are also very well paid. This system is sharply criticized in France, but it does facilitate the recruitment of talented men.

Patterns of career mobility

How do the careers of the highest civil servants develop? What process determines the movement from one post to another? What is the importance of such mobility? These are the issues I will explore next.

The French system is influenced by two factors that are often interrelated but that must be distinguished in order to analyze them: the role of the ministerial cabinets in career advancement, and mobility patterns that differ according to administrative categories.

Nominations to the higher posts are achieved often in an unsystematic manner, after one or more stints in a ministerial cabinet. The age at which higher civil servants enter the cabinets varies according to the function performed: technical counselors, the men at the interior of the cabinets who are directly associated with the definition of policies and programs, are usually thirty to forty-five years old; cabinet heads are forty-five to fifty. The choice of particular individuals is made through personal contacts and friendships, or on the recommendations of department directors, according to the requests of the ministers or cabinet heads.

Working in a ministerial cabinet provides the higher civil servant with the opportunity to apprentice at the very heart of government. He enlarges his horizon, adds important psychological and political factors to his perspective, and becomes familiar with the practical mechanisms of decisionmaking.

After having exercised his duties for from one to three years, a cabinet member is appointed to a position signifying an advancement in his career. Ministers' associates are appointed as department directors or as managers of public establishments or national enterprises relevant to a particular department. Counselors to the president or the prime minister are appointed to the most varied posts within the domains in which they operate.

Nominations and promotions granted after a time spent in a ministerial cabinet operate to the benefit not only of higher civil servants who come from a ministry and stay in it but also of those who want a chance to leave their original ministry or corps for another. Horizontal or interministerial mobility is thus possible.

The promotion of members of ministerial cabinets permits relatively young men to occupy some of the highest posts in the French government. This is particularly true of financial inspectors and mining engineers. (However, not all nominations to important posts are reserved for members of ministerial cabinets, and sometimes a ministerial cabinet member will return to his agency without a promotion.)

Administrative mobility in the higher civil service is an old tradition in France. Under the monarchy higher civil servants who acted as counselors to the king were often emissaries who had represented him in the provinces. During the First Empire, members of the Council of State often left their duties to perform varied special tasks. During the nineteenth century, this practice benefited such groups as financial inspectors and engineers from the School of Mines and the School of Bridges and Roads. The custom accelerated after 1945 and even more so after 1958, as growing state intervention created a large number of new public bodies whose directors were, in a quasi-systematic manner, chosen from the corps of higher civil servants. (One exception was Jean Monnet, the businessman who was appointed planning commissioner in 1946.)

In France the "zone of mobility," that is, the arena within which the transfers of higher civil servants from one position to another are made, is vast. It covers virtually all of the state apparatus except for the Department of Defense.

The movement of personnel primarily occurs between positions located within the capital: the office of the prime minister, ministries, administrative bodies, large public establishments, and national enterprises. It extends, but in a lesser degree, to field services (prefectures, general treasuries, regional and departmental extensions of ministries) and to offices outside the national territories (embassies and international organizations).

French higher civil servants can work temporarily outside the national government: in private enterprises, in universities, or in local governments. (There are twenty-five *énarques,* graduates of the ENA, working for the city of Paris as well as fifty or so members of the prefectorial body in the service of various regional or departmental assemblies.) Civil servants can also become parliamentarians or run for ministerial office without giving up their administrative careers.

The nature of the tasks performed by higher civil servants who are transferred from one post to another merits examination. In the simplest case, the duties of the new job are similar to those that were previously exercised: an administrator in the Budget Office is named the director of finance for some public enterprise, or an engineer from the Bureau of Bridges and Roads is named to the division of the Ministry of National Education responsible for building schools. In the second case, the individual's duties are larger and more diversified: a civil administrator or financial inspector working in the Treasury Division of the Department of Economy and Finance is named director of a public bank or a state insurance company. In the third case, the successive responsibilities are very different. Two examples: Marceau Long, a member of the Council of State, was, successively, the secretary general for administration in the Department of Defense, director general of the National Radio-Television Company, secretary general of the government, and president of the national airlines, Air-Inter; Paul Delouvrier, a financial inspector, was a financial expert in the Planning Commissariat, deputy director of tax collection, general director of the Commission of the European Community in Brussels, French delegate to Algeria, prefect of the region around Paris, and finally president of the French national electric power company.

The cases of Long and Delouvrier are admittedly out of the ordinary, but there are many examples of French higher civil servants who have occupied two or even three positions of responsibility in different domains during their careers.

Civil servants in certain departments (for example, the Department of Economy and Finance or the Department of Industry) or in the *grands corps* move frequently. The most typical case is that of the Inspectorate General of Finance, where nine out of ten members hold positions outside the department. Inversely, certain ministries are "permanent importers" of civil servants: Labor, Health, Culture, Tourism, Cooperation, Environment, and Youth and Sports, to name a few. Other ministries (Post and Telecommunications, Justice, and Defense) live in relative autarchy: they import few people and export even fewer.

Civil servants who move from state agencies to public enterprises often move back again. Thus members of the Council of State or the Audit Agency exercise "detached" responsibilities in organs outside their own departments and, after a few years, return to the fold to finish out their careers. It is the same, though less frequent, for certain engineers in the Departments of Mining or of Bridges and Roads.

On the other hand, for many higher civil servants, emigration is permanent. They end their careers in an outside department, or, after several years spent in service to the state, in a public or private enterprise.[7] This is true for the majority of financial inspectors and for many mining engineers and graduates of the Ecole Polytechnique. By 1982 some 150 to 200 of the 3,000 alumni of the ENA were employed in private businesses. (They were even more numerous until the socialist government nationalized many of the private industrial firms and banks whose key posts had been filled by *énarques*.)

While mobility among higher civil servants is frequent, it is neither systematic nor universal. In many ministries, administra-

7. The practice in French is called *pantouflage,* from *pantoufle* (slipper).

tors spend all or the major portion of their careers within the department in which they entered government service. For this reason the government decided in 1964 that all former students of the ENA should undergo a two-year period of mandatory mobility within four years of having graduated. The transfers were to be to completely different departments.

Generalists and specialists

In the French system both generalists (administrative and scientific) and specialists are important. Let me examine each category in turn.

Before 1945 all administrative generalists were graduates of the Free School of Political Science or a school of law. They were recruited by competitive written examinations and their training program included a number of specific courses. Though each department and specialized body had its own entrance exam, all of them were intended to seek out people with a knowledge of the humanities, an aptitude for logical reasoning, oral and written communications skills, some legal knowledge or experience, and, to a lesser degree, training in administration or public finance.

After 1945 the specific exams were superseded. Future administrative generalists entered the ENA after completing their education at the Paris Institute of Political Studies (which replaced the Free School). These *énarques* were not exactly the same as their predecessors. A knowledge of literature and history remained vital, as did the ability to write and speak clearly and vigorously. But legal expertise became less important and the study of government administration and economic and social policy (both in France and in other Western European nations) became more so. There has also been an added emphasis on modern management methods.

Over the past twenty-eight years, the courses leading to an ENA degree have been modified several times. Emphasis at one time was placed on the unity of education, at another time on the necessity of instituting common courses as well as certain rather specialized ones (general administration, economics, social policies, and international affairs).

After receiving a degree from the ENA, students are sent to a department (Economy and Finance, Foreign Affairs, Education, and so on) or to an interdepartmental corps (Council of State, Audit Agency, Inspectorate General of Finance). Here they work in a particular post and acquire a specialized expertise. Certain of them will continue in their careers; others quit after five or ten years.

Administrative generalists in France thus do not constitute a homogeneous class. There is initially a common base among the higher civil servants who possess an ENA degree; but after a few years, the practical skills that they acquire in the course of their work, the intellectual methods and values of each administration, and the perspectives gleaned from their professional activities give each of them a different profile.

The general pattern is the same for scientific generalists, who receive a common education at one of the *grandes écoles*, completed by a specialization in a technical school (School of Mines, School of Bridges and Roads, School of Weapons and Arms, School of Telecommunications, School of Statistics and Economic Administration, and so on).[8] This training is not intended to create specialized engineers in the different fields of technology nor graduates who immediately put their knowledge to use in a factory or research department. Its object is to provide administrators with a scientific or mathematical background who will be able to exercise the responsibilities of management *and* be capable of communicating with engineers and specialized technicians.

It must be stressed here that scientific generalists are not groomed solely for the purpose of working for governmental, civil, or military organs; the degrees that they acquire also lead them to industrial, public, semi-public, or private enterprises. This is one important difference between them and the graduates of the ENA, whose program is exclusively oriented toward public administration.

The education received by the technicians (called Xs) has changed over the course of the last twenty-five years. Some of this is due to changes in the sciences themselves and some to an effort to make the Xs better understand the problems of fundamental research, which they have had a tendency to neglect. Today scientific generalists also acquire a much deeper understanding of economics, particularly mathematical economics. Certain of them follow management programs, often at an American university or business school. Finally, the *grandes écoles* and the various vocational schools are anxious to maintain a high level in the humanities, communications, and the human sciences.

After leaving the technical schools, scientific generalists are posted to various departments: mining engineers to the Department of Industry; construction engineers to the Departments of Transportation and Construction; statisticians to the Department

8. These schools are called *écoles d'applications* and are separate from the Ecole Polytechnique.

of Economy and Finance; military engineers to the Department of Defense; and agricultural engineers to the Department of Agriculture. Like the *énarques,* they rapidly acquire a special mind set. After ten or fifteen years, the former Xs no longer have exactly the same profiles.

What positions do generalists occupy in the French government? The paradigm is very complicated, but it is governed by practices that normally permit generalists to know their career prospects. Depending on their preferences and on the department to which they belong, they can orient their professional ambitions toward an area in which they have a reasonable chance for success.

Generally speaking, the system is such that certain sectors are reserved for each family or category of higher civil servant. This system of "guarded inroads" is not applied in any systematic fashion, however: a certain number of positions or sectors can be occupied by higher civil servants of different origins.

Several positions in the state apparatus are traditionally reserved for administrative generalists (that is to say, ENA graduates). This is the case for positions in the *secrétariat génèral du gouvernment,* the permanent staff that assists the prime minister. It is also usually the case for directors, deputy directors, and the like in departments such as Economy and Finance, Interior, and Foreign Affairs.

Within the family of administrative generalists are certain subdivisions, each of which "possesses" areas in which it occupies either an exclusive or a predominant position. The Inspectorate General of Finance, for example, has very strong positions at the heart of the Department of Economy and Finance and in the financial institutions on which they depend, such as the banks.

The situation is more or less the same for scientific generalists. Graduates of the *grandes écoles* attain many positions in departments, general establishments of the state, and national enterprises. In some they occupy all, or the majority, of the key posts. Within the family of scientific generalists, there are subdivisions holding monopolies or dominant positions in certain organizations. Mining engineers are numerous in the departments or organs charged with geologic research, the coal industry, metallurgy and iron works, the oil industry, and nuclear research. Construction engineers often work in the areas of transportation, hydraulics, electricity, construction, urban planning, civil engineering, and so on.

There definitely exists in the French upper administration two relatively stable "delimited territories" that share administrative and scientific generalists. But there is no firm barrier between these two zones of influence. Certain key positions are alternately occupied by men coming from one or the other group, and frequently a staff dominated by one family of generalists has a few members of the other family. Some *énarques* currently work in agencies or public enterprises dominated by Xs (for example, in certain sections of the Department of Transportation, in the oil division of the Ministry of Industry, and in the French railways). Conversely, Xs occupy some posts in the Departments of Economy and Finance, External Affairs, and Education. Finally, certain students of the Polytechnique continue on to the ENA after their graduation, which permits them to enter the *grands corps* as part of the Council of State.

The preceding developments have concentrated on the *énarques* and on the Xs. One should not forget that certain key positions in the French upper administration are occupied by people from a different background: university professors (in the Department of Education and elsewhere), judges (in the Department of Justice), and doctors (in the Department of Health). But one must recognize that their numbers are limited and that these specialists are frequently placed under the authority of generalists.

In-service training

In France there is no centralized or organized system designed to develop the professional capacities of higher civil servants after their entry into the administration. The need for a continuing education program for career administrators was recognized toward the end of the Second World War, and in 1945 the government decided to create a center of higher administrative studies, which was separate from the ENA.[9] Despite some interesting results, the project was abandoned after a dozen years. An attempt to revive it—a plan proposed in the 1960s by State Counselor Pierre Laroque for "perfecting the civil service"—was rejected by the government.

The difficulties encountered in devising an in-service training system are numerous. If the courses were mandatory (for example, necessary for a promotion), they could be considered a constraint or a formality. If they were optional, they might not be attended by the higher civil servants who really needed them. There is also the question of how to define the contents of the new educational programs and how to make them respond to the varied needs of higher civil servants. Experience shows, for example, that the levels are very different for various personnel, depending on their

9. Though the two schools were separate, they were managed by the same director and housed in the same building.

age and the positions that they have held. Moreover, the training sessions often have as a goal initiating the students to new techniques or new methodologies. But there is always the danger of a great separation between what is being taught and what the students find upon return to their positions. Finally, in a country where civil servants are already highly educated, it is difficult to find speakers and lecturers of an equivalent or superior level.

Within the last twenty years, numerous sessions have been organized both inside and outside the government to discuss the major fields, policies, and "common problems" of higher civil servants (computers, statistics, management, public contracts, human relations, and so on). In certain departments, the conferences are mandatory for the younger higher civil servants; in others participation is a matter of individual interest and initiative (even if the offices are willing to pay all expenses).

Some higher civil servants strive to use what they learn at conferences and from professional journals, or what they glean by working for certain exterior organs, such as the French Institute of Administrative Sciences. Thanks to this institute, and other similar organizations, they can confer with university professors in public administration and public policy.

One might hope that in France the participation of higher civil servants in such groups would enable them to expand their knowledge and to deepen their understanding of contemporary problems. Unfortunately, there is no overall, centralized, consistent effort to provide administrators, at all the stages of their careers, with chances to improve their performance.

Conclusion

What overall judgments can be made about the relations between politicians and the higher civil service in France?

The French system does have some definite advantages. It places in important government positions men and women who not only are dynamic but also know how to manipulate the bureaucratic machinery. Thus ever since the beginning of the Fifth Republic, a new type of leader has emerged: a higher civil servant interested above all in carrying out a program. Having inside knowledge of the administrative environment, the manager minister is in a better position to obtain results.[10] Moreover, the French system enables the president, the prime minister, and the cabinet ministers to be assisted by officials whom they have chosen

10. Michel Debré is the most characteristic example of the politician who is action oriented and who emerged from the higher civil service. One might also cite Olivier Guichard, Albin Chalandon, Edgar Pisani, Jacques Duhamel, and André Giraud.

with great freedom, officials who are loyal but who at the same time have considerable government experience. These officials, ambitious and self-confident, work with the ministerial staff or at the senior managerial level in carrying out new programs. They are often considered arrogant, but they are quite effective.[11]

French centralization and the old tradition of the omnipresent and interventionist state offer politicians and administrators possibilities for action and fulfillment superior to those that can be found in many other countries. In France the central government can intervene directly in local affairs by acting in conjunction with the local assemblies or at their request, and the central government does not hesitate to impose its will.

Ever since the end of the Second World War, and even more so since the beginning of the Fifth Republic, the French government has often used the approach of the "program-oriented agency" or the "project-oriented staff," a procedure that was partly inspired by the American Tennessee Valley Authority. Established by the government, managed by officials of diverse origins coming from the senior levels of the civil service, the program-oriented agencies have some notable successes to their credit.

Have governmental and administrative authorities been able to fully use the instrumentalities described above to achieve their objectives?

In the economic area, the answer is yes. There have been noteworthy results in productivity improvement, industry optimization, and, more generally, growth assistance; in oil policy; in transportation infrastructure; in construction of nuclear power plants; and in developing less-advanced French regions.

In other sectors—social welfare, medical assistance distribution, education, and environmental, cultural, and leisure improvement—the results have been only average and seem more or less comparable to those in the majority of European countries.

In still other areas the steps taken by the public sector have produced minimal results: the fight against inflation, fiscal reform, foreign worker programs, and campaigns against alcoholism and for reductions in road accidents. Some programs have failed completely (certain industrial and technological development schemes), while others have even ended in scandal (the reconstruction of the Villette slaughterhouse in Paris).

11. Jérôme Monod, a collaborator of Michel Debré's at the prime minister's residence and later a delegate to Territorial Management, was long considered the prototype of the young and aggressive "winner" technocrat.

This shows that no administrative instrumentalities can be miraculous. Decision processes get results only if managed by men who are ambitious, rational, and skillful. Success cannot be achieved without the support of public opinion and influential groups.

Is the political and administrative system in France more easily understood, better organized, and more consistent than that of other Western industrial countries? Yes and no.

It is undeniable that the preponderant role played in the operation of government institutions by generalists with legal and managerial backgrounds contributes to unification of the system: French higher civil servants speak the same language. Further, mobility creates personal bonds among the personnel posted to different ministries, and information circulates more smoothly among government agencies. French methods no doubt permit a more ready response to a need present in all states, the need to "maintain lateral coordination among interdependent programs."[12]

Unfortunately, there are elements of the French system that lend themselves to disorder: the individuality, somewhat anarchical, of the higher civil service (there is more discipline, it would appear, in British and German administration); the tendency of each administration to surround itself with rigid barriers; and the intramural rivalries of the higher civil service.

French higher civil servants come for the most part from the more favored social strata. This situation can be explained to a large extent by the important role played in the system by generalists. They are necessarily recruited by a competitive examination of a high intellectual level. Young people from the lower classes are still scarce at French universities: in addition, those who are there seem to prefer teaching and the scientific or technical professions.

It is therefore difficult to broaden the social recruitment of high-level administrators. To meet this objective it would be necessary to democratize not only higher education but also the more elite sections of the senior high school classes. It would also be necessary to change social attitudes.

Are the values, beliefs, and attitudes of high French administrative officials characteristic of an elite and therefore antithetical to the aspirations of the nation as a whole? Are these officials more insulated from the social and cultural realities of their country than their counterparts in other European countries?

12. Douglas E. Ashford, *Policy and Politics in France: Living with Uncertainty* (Temple University Press, 1982), p. 56.

This criticism is often heard, but an adequate answer would require a much more detailed discussion than is possible here. High career officials, in France as well as in Great Britain, the Federal Republic of Germany, and Sweden, occupy positions of authority: their horizons, of course, cannot be the same as those of the individuals subject to that authority. But it does not seem that the values that they share, that have been analyzed so well by foreign observers, are very different from those of the majority of Frenchmen.

The Higher Civil Service in Europe and the United States

JAMES W. FESLER

THREE background features help to explain the difficulty of exporting civil service institutions from one country to another, and especially from Europe to the United States. If these seem commonplace, it is partly because I choose not to bog myself down in the quagmire of differences in "national character," despite its renewed respectability under the rubric of "national culture." Of the many possible differentiating features, I chose the public sector's share of the economy, the proportion of people employed by the national government as compared with all public employees and with the population as a whole, and the systems of higher education.

In the late 1970s total government expenditures in Germany, France, and Britain amounted to about 45 percent of the gross domestic product (GDP); in the United States, the figure was only 33 percent of GDP. In fact, by this measure, the United States ranked sixteenth among the nineteen nations surveyed by the Organization for Economic Cooperation and Development.[1] The United States has no tradition of *étatisme* or *dirigisme*.

In contrast to the French practice, but as in Germany and Canada, the U.S. federal government employs only a small percentage (18 percent) of all government employees. This percentage of federal employees has steadily declined since World War II as state and local employment rose. Federal employment also has declined in relation to population—from 166 federal employees per 10,000 people in 1952 to 118 in 1981. The United States thus has had to do more with proportionately fewer federal employees; the actual number has remained between 2.8 million and 2.9 million since 1969.[2] These numbers also show that the federal government is relying more on state and local governments

1. David R. Cameron, "On the Limits of the Public Economy," *Annals of the American Academy of Political and Social Science,* vol. 459 (January 1982), p. 49.

2. U.S. Advisory Commission on Intergovernmental Relations, *Significant Features of Fiscal Federalism, 1981–82 Edition,* Report M-35 (Washington, D.C.: ACIR, 1983), pp. 72ff.

to implement national policies (and on private and quasi-private enterprises to police themselves). Yet whereas German federal agencies engage almost entirely in policy formation, the U.S. government directly administers large national programs and it extensively regulates and monitors state and local governments' execution of federally initiated programs.

Finally, one should bear in mind the contrasts among the higher educational systems of the five countries discussed in this volume, particularly in the educational experiences of those destined for high civil service posts. A general concern is the degree of social bias governing admission to and survival at relevant institutions of higher education. More particular concerns are the German stress on legal training, the weakness of French universities compared with the *grandes écoles,* the British reliance on Oxford and Cambridge, and the Canadian and American recruitment from a wide range of colleges and universities. (According to one survey, no single institution accounted for more than 4 percent of the B.A. degrees held by top U.S. careerists.)

Now let me turn to our proper subject and speak to the two issues that seem most relevant.

First, the greatest contrast between the higher civil service in the United States and those in Europe and Canada lies in the number of top political appointments in relation to the number of top career civil service positions. The fragility of boundary definitions for each country's high-political, high-career, and lower-level employees makes precise counts elusive, but that qualifies only marginally the gross comparisons I am making.

New administrations in Britain and France make 100 top political appointments; a new group in power in Germany makes about 80;[3] a change in the White House, however, can result in 1,400 new political appointments. Since the United States has about 7,500 top career posts, the ratio of high-political to high-career officials is 1:5. The British and French ratios, in contrast, are 1:40, and the German ratio is 1:80.

The large number of political appointments in the United States obviously increases the likelihood of less-than-discriminating selections by a newly elected president and his cabinet. But there are other less apparent problems. The United States has no shadow cabinet, informed and ready to take over the running of departments; it also has no permanent secretaries as in Britain, no career

3. For details on the calculation of the European political echelons, see James W. Fesler, "The Higher Public Service in Western Europe," in Ralph Clark Chandler, ed., *A Centennial History of the American Administrative State* (Wiley, forthcoming).

deputy ministers as in Canada, no ministerial cabinets with 70 percent careerist membership as in France, and no tenured state secretaries as in Germany. When an administration changes, each department is more than beheaded; the displacement of incumbents runs through several layers of the hierarchical pyramid, down to deputy assistant secretaries, bureau chiefs, regional directors, and others. Often as many as 50 to 175 officials of a department may be replaced. This interruption in continuity is not limited to the beginning of a new administration. The tenure of political executives is usually so short, averaging about two years, and so noncongruent that each department's team of leaders is in a constant state of flux. As Hugh Heclo so aptly put it, we have "a government of strangers."[4] I know of no comparable phenomenon in Europe, even though some ministers, certainly in France and Britain, have short tenures.

One consequence is that top American careerists have much less contact with department heads than do the political executives at subcabinet and sub-subcabinet levels. James Sundquist has shown that American careerists have a lesser role than their European counterparts in high-level policy formation.[5] Another consequence is that, with so many new and inexperienced people above them, top careerists must develop political sensitivities and strategies protective of their programs. This helps to explain why careerists have as much contact with Congress and with organized interest groups as do political executives.[6]

The relation of American careerists to political authorities is complex. It reflects the constitutional system of separation of powers and checks and balances, the organization of Congress, and the adaptation of interest groups to these formal features. Four points may be made. First, Congress has at least as much constitutional authority over administration as does the president. Second, Congress organizes itself in specialized committees and subcommittees, whose members and staff aides develop considerable expertise about individual agencies and programs. Their knowledge and range of policy views and those of the careerists are well matched. As Aberbach, Putnam, and Rockman put it, "The bureaucrats and politicians [legislators] across the hearing-

4. Hugh Heclo, *A Government of Strangers: Executive Politics in Washington* (Brookings Institution, 1977).

5. James L. Sundquist, "A Comparison of Policymaking Capacity in the United States and Five European Countries," in Michael E. Kraft and Mark Schneider, eds., *Population Policy Analysis* (Heath, 1978), pp. 67–80.

6. Joel D. Aberbach, Robert D. Putnam, and Bert A. Rockman, *Bureaucrats and Politicians in Western Democracies* (Harvard University Press, 1981), pp. 230ff.

room tables of Washington have much more in common than would be true in Paris, or Rome, or London, or even Bonn."[7] Third, agency and program issues typically attract the symbiotic involvement of agencies, relevant committees, and concerned interest groups, as well as of specialized policy networks extending inside and outside government. Fourth, if members of such combinations are mutually supportive, as symbiotic organisms often are, an agency can develop substantial autonomy vis-à-vis the departmental and presidential hierarchy. Many conclude that this fragmentation has led to a "balkanized" executive branch, in which segments of a major problem are dealt with piecemeal and with a short time frame, at the expense of broader, long-range planning.

European countries do possess organized interest groups with access to administrative agencies, and there are complaints about the autonomy of individual units—for instance, the *directions* in France. But in that instance, the ministerial cabinet within each ministry is a counterweight to such autonomy: being staffed mostly with civil servants, it presumably takes into account more long-range and general-interest considerations than does an American department with its short-lived political appointees.

If political-career relations (especially appointment ratios) are the first major contrast between the European and the U.S. systems, the second most significant lies in the specialist-versus-generalist traditions (together with mobility and career patterns). All European countries emphasize, in varying degrees, the generalist tradition. The members of the British administrative class (surviving without the name) are the most clearly in this tradition, retaining an effective monopoly of decisionmaking authority despite the post-Fulton infusion of economists and scientists at high levels. Members of the French *grands corps,* even those who are graduates of the Polytechnique and of specialized engineering schools, often spend only two years in their specialized ministries and thereafter rove elsewhere, capitalizing on their claims to polyvalence. They are specialists in generalization. Because of the *Länders'* special administrative role, most top federal careerists in Germany are absorbed in policy and belong to the general administrative service (though, as in the United States, they develop special competence and mostly pursue careers in a single ministry). In Britain and France, the movement of able careerists among positions and ministries is common, though France better

7. Ibid., p. 243.

manages interministerial careers through the attentiveness of the grand masters of the *grands corps*. In both countries, young careerists qualifying as "high flyers" are especially mobile.

The specialist tradition dominates the U.S. civil service. Civil servants are recruited as specialists, and their service on the way up is confined to a single bureau or, certainly, department. This is true even though their responsibilities are increasingly of a broad policy and administrative character, involving interaction with other political and administrative power centers. One clue, a contrast to Europe, is that the university majors of 42 percent of the top civil servants were in technology and the natural sciences.[8] Interdepartmental mobility is rare; it is more common among staff people than among program administrators, and it is dependent mostly on the initiative of civil servants themselves.

This is not to say that American civil servants have not risen to high posts that require general administrative abilities unrelated to their university specialization or that some have not gone beyond single-bureau careers. But few of these have been young "high flyers"; they are more likely to be lateral entrants near the top. A surprising number of careerists have accepted political appointments as assistant secretaries, though this typically has meant the loss of their civil service status. Presidents often make such choices in the waning years or months of an administration, when private-sector candidates are scarce. From the 1930s on, the United States has made various attempts to introduce modifications of the British administrative class model. The latest effort, though a far cry from that model, is the Senior Executive Service, established by statute in 1978, which is intended to facilitate flexible assignments for political and career officials alike. So far, though, the service seems not to have promoted interdepartmental mobility.

Concluding, I feel despair and hope. I have been struck by the eagerness with which reformists in all our countries, since at least 1870, have acidly criticized their own higher public services and have sought to import major features of other countries' civil service systems. I have been equally struck by the failure of most such importation efforts to win acceptance, or, if adopted, to escape unintended consequences. The result is a set of national systems that remain remarkably distinct.

The most distinctive features of the U.S. public service have been the high proportion of political appointments, the tradition

8. Ibid., p. 52.

of specialized recruitment and career paths, and, related to these features, the discontinuity in leadership at the levels where administration and policy converge. I believe that our priorities should be to reduce the number of political posts and to strengthen executive-development programs aimed at preparing rising, specialized careerists for the broader roles they will be expected to perform.

Lessons for the United States

DAVID T. STANLEY

FORMIDABLE difficulties of several kinds must be overcome if the United States is to draw useful lessons from the experiences of other nations with their higher civil services. First and most obvious are the differences from country to country. Great Britain, Canada, France, Germany, and the United States differ in political history, structure, and culture. All but the United States have a parliamentary form of government, with its intertwining of legislative and executive work. Three of the five countries are federal; two are unitary. Transitions among the ruling parties vary in their frequency and in their effects on the different bureaucracies, as does the degree of popular and political regard for the public service. Economic problems have greater or lesser impact on the public services of the five nations. Both the United States and the United Kingdom have made concerted efforts to reduce government expenditures, particularly domestic social spending. Executive style is a further variable. Ronald Reagan and Margaret Thatcher have been less than complimentary in remarks about their bureaucracies, and both have cut resources for administrative sustenance. Finally, the bureaucracies themselves differ from one country to another in their composition (social, ethnic, educational), in their traditional behavior and attitudes, and in their political strength. For all these reasons, and probably more, policymakers in the United States have been unwilling or unable to adopt the positive features of the higher civil service systems of other countries. In Professor Fesler's phrase, "Much of what we have heard is not readily exportable."

A second type of difficulty is simply how the problems are perceived, even by experts. Some readers may have wondered if the writers of these papers were all at the same meeting; this is the old problem of differences in the reports of witnesses to alleged miracles or actual accidents—this conference being something in between.

Another difficulty is the question of who in the United States

93

needs to learn the lessons—and who is willing to try to apply them.

Having set up all these obstacles, I now clamber over them to review what has been and can be learned and done as a result of this Brookings conference. The topics are those framed by the conference planners and followed by the authors of the papers presented.

Relations between bureaucrats and politicians

Lesson A: The higher civil service needs and deserves to be treated with respect and appreciation.

Political leaders in the United States, reflecting to some degree the antibureaucratic cultural tradition of our country, have, particularly in recent administrations, joked about or denigrated the civil service. President Carter and President Reagan have both acted as though the civil service were an adversary rather than part of their own team. A similar attitude is now visible in Great Britain, but not, on the whole, in the other countries represented at this conference. The cure is a concentrated effort by more enlightened political leaders, the academic community, and the media to emphasize the positive achievements and difficult tasks of the senior levels of the bureaucracy. It may be that the attitudinal pendulum will swing in the United States; indeed it is likely that most of the avowed candidates for president, with the exception of the incumbent, will show signs of learning this lesson.

Lesson B: Higher civil servants can and should make major contributions to policy planning and development.

This lesson is closely related to the previous one. If the political leadership respects the knowledge and experience of the senior career staff, the latter will be used to comment on proposed legislation or policy choices. This does not mean that the higher civil service will dominate policymaking, as has been reported in some of the other countries, since politically appointed officials will still dictate and dominate policy decisions in the United States. There has been a tendency, particularly in the last two administrations, for executives who are not part of the incoming political team to have little share in decisionmaking. This, however, is still *only* a tendency, and there is probably much more consultation actually going on than is publicly acknowledged. After all, it is the career bureaucracy that keeps the figures, understands the background, and can warn against legal tangles when new courses of action are being considered.

Such consultation should be facilitated by the functioning of the Senior Executive Service, established by the Civil Service

Reform Act of 1978. This law recognizes what other countries have already learned: that career higher civil servants should be able to move with or be selected by their political superiors, so that they can work with persons whose administrative styles and, to some extent, political and economic views are compatible with their own—without losing tenure in the process.

It is possible in the United States, as in other countries, for higher civil servants to move into politically appointive positions and for political officials (normally in the lower levels) to shift to career-type jobs.

Lesson C: There is already an informal cadre of "public careerists" who, in effect, constitute an auxiliary higher civil service even though they are politically appointed.

Previous papers have reported that there are similar officials in France and Germany, and that these "in-and-outers" are a valuable source of knowledge and experience. We have learned in our own country to be careful that the appointment of such persons does not violate conflict-of-interest laws or other ethical principles, but this barrier is on the whole understood and dealt with.

Lesson D: There probably should be a higher percentage of career civil servants compared to politically appointed officials in policymaking positions in the U.S. government.

This is a debatable issue, and no clearcut proportion can be specified. However, there has been a deplorable tendency in American government to appoint a layer of political under secretaries, beneath that a layer of political assistant secretaries, and beneath that a layer of deputy assistant secretaries. Thus one must penetrate several echelons downward to find the repository of experience and data necessary for decisionmaking. Of course, many political appointees learn quickly and adapt well to the job of assisting their department heads with administration, policy-making, and appearances on Capitol Hill, but there needs to be a greater leavening of career experience at the levels cited. This is much more easily said than done, because of the strong pressure to give political appointments to deserving people who have worked on the campaigns or have performed other services.

Self-administration in the civil service

Lesson A: The initiative of higher civil servants and decisions by department heads are already major factors in the assignment of members of the higher civil service.

All of the countries represented at this conference acknowledge that the wishes and willingness of civil servants themselves have much to do with their acceptance of the posts to which they are appointed. All of the countries except Germany have central personnel organizations to provide recordkeeping, planning, service, and support for the civil service; actual decisions on personnel movement, however, are normally made by the employing ministries.

In the United States the central machinery consists of the Office of Personnel Management (OPM), responsible for leadership, standard-setting, program evaluation, and some approvals; the Merit Systems Protection Board, for appeals decisions, other program evaluations, and detection of irregularities; and the White House, the Office of Management and Budget (OMB), and Congress, all responsible for basic policy and for the determination of pay and benefits. Employment and assignment decisions are made by the department heads concerned.

Lesson B: The Office of Personnel Management could perform a more important service in program planning, training and development, and mobility assignments.

Although assignments and promotions are generally managed by the employing departments in the five countries represented here, there is a greater recognition in Europe and Canada of the value of interministry movement and formal staff development. The fact that American agency heads have the power of appointment has contributed to a feeling of possessiveness that limits interagency mobility and discourages the assignment of the more promising higher civil servants to formal training institutions. Program managers seem much more concerned with getting work done than with developing staff. This is an unarguable priority, but much more emphasis needs to be placed on assignments for developmental purposes. The OPM should play a bigger part in planning development programs and in arranging for interagency placements.

Mobility and career patterns

Lesson A: Several U.S. government agencies have a strong tradition of developmental assignment programs for higher civil servants; such programs should be encouraged and promoted government-wide.

Among the agencies that conduct effective executive development programs for career staff are the Internal Revenue Service, the National Park Service, the Social Security Administration, the Veterans Administration, the Forest Service, the Army Corps of Engineers, and the Foreign Service (not a part of the regular civil service). All of these have used interbureau and interregional assignments for developmental purposes. Many other departments and agencies, however, still lack significant developmental programs, and strong leadership by the White House, the OMB, and the OPM—all of which have statutory leadership responsibilities—should move toward the objective of the Civil Service Reform Act in planning and conducting such programs for career personnel. This cannot be done without leadership from the very top of the government or without a heightened appreciation of the importance of a top-quality career bureaucrat. The president should make clear his desire that such programs be carried out and adequately funded; the OMB should follow through, and the OPM should provide guidance and standards as well as verify program quality.

Lesson B: Incentives and machinery are needed to encourage interagency movement among career higher civil servants.

Although the other countries represented at this conference reported that members of their higher civil services tended to serve largely in one ministry, a number of very useful examples were cited of outstanding public servants who had been moved from one ministry to another. In the U.S. government this occurs primarily on the initiative of the individual employee and is rarely, if ever, part of a systematic plan of development. Such interagency movement need not be compulsory or artificial, but incentives could be offered and planning could be directed toward encouraging mobility and the transfer of useful experience from one agency to another. This would avoid the tendency of higher civil servants who spend all or most of their careers in one agency to become advocates for that agency and possible adversaries of others. Developmental transfers and promotions among kindred agencies would work against such a parochial attitude and would result in a broadened perspective for the higher civil servants concerned.

Interagency executive mobility would be particularly desirable among groups of agencies with common types of functions, for example, law enforcement, utilization of natural resources, or environmental protection. The career development of civil engineers, for instance, could be enriched by interchange between the Army Corps of Engineers and the Bureau of Reclamation. Similar arrangements could be made for recreation specialists or foresters between the Forest Service and the Park Service. Even broader interagency mobility could be arranged for experts in general administration. And purely federal mobility could be further enhanced by interchanges between the legislative and executive branches, or between federal agencies and counterpart functional offices in state and local governments.

Specialists versus generalists, and in-service training

Lesson A: The generalist tradition in Europe and the specialist tradition in the United States have both been exaggerated. The use of "broadened specialists" seems to be increasing.

During this conference representatives from the United Kingdom reported increased emphasis on the use of specialists, but they maintained that the generalist tradition was still strong, particularly because it served to produce persons who were useful to ministers in planning legislation, answering questions in the House of Commons, and performing other duties. (Many U.S. government officials perform similar duties, whether they are politically appointed or part of the career service; in other European countries officials tend to specialize, but they take on broader assignments as their careers progress.)

It may be time to stop speaking of specialists and generalists, and to emphasize instead what may be called a "broad stream" concept, under which experts with experience in the administration of scientific programs, professionals well acquainted with financial markets, specialists in dealing with contract and procurement functions, and experts in law enforcement will be recruited on the basis of appropriate education. Once in the service, they will proceed through a program of planned assignments, supplemented by appropriate course work either within the federal service or at appropriate universities, as part of their progress toward top-level positions in appropriate functional areas.

Lesson B: Formalized executive training facilities must continue to be developed.

The U.S. Federal Executive Institute (FEI) has long served as a central facility for short courses for executives from a variety of organizations. The FEI is roughly comparable to the British Civil Service College, the German Federal Academy for Public Administration, and the French National School of Administration. The FEI's work is supplemented by OPM's executive seminar centers, which offer short-term courses at lower levels. In addition, other federal agencies occasionally send senior employees to seminars or even full-year courses in professional specialities, or public affairs, or administration.

Nevertheless, more political and budgetary support is needed. The Federal Executive Institute nearly went out of business about two years ago, and was saved from extinction only by concerted bureaucratic and political pressure. One problem was that the FEI could not find enough mid-career students, a dilemma faced by other professional schools of public administration and non-profit educational institutions. And one reason for this difficulty was that in the federal government the most promising employees tended to be kept on the job, while those who were more easily spared were released for training.

As noted earlier, there is also a need for more planned development through work assignments (and for work assignments to be available when training is over). The Presidential Management Intern Program has been effective in the development of administrative generalists, but in the last year or two it has been difficult to find enough positions for the promising young people in the program.

All this is in stark contrast to the American corporate world, where executive development is seen as a major management responsibility. Again, the solution lies in stronger political support (from the White House on down through the ranks of the federal bureaucracy), adequate funding from OMB, and the selection and retention of development-minded top executives.

Pay as an incentive

The conference devoted some spirited discussion to the issue of compensation for higher civil servants, even though this was not one of the major topics up for review. Our conclusion was that higher civil servants are motivated as much by appreciation and encouragement from the political leadership and by recognition of the important public service they perform as by monetary compensation.

Repeated studies of the U.S. federal civil service show that salary is no more than a secondary or tertiary form of motivation for performance. What primarily motivates executives is the importance of the service they are rendering and the recognition of that fact by their superiors and the public. Pay is, of course, one form of recognition. Compensation policies that permit higher civil servants to be reasonably and regularly rewarded, even if their salaries are not competitive with those in the private sector, have generally been adequate to maintain effective management leadership. The decline in the morale of the Senior Executive Service is attributable only in part to the fact that no pay increases were possible for a number of years; more important were the denunciations of the civil service by the political leadership, the feeling among many civil servants that the political superiors to whom they reported were unable to provide proper leadership, and the depressing effects of lower budgets and resultant reductions in staffs.

Bonus programs for members of the Senior Executive Service and merit pay provisions for managers in grades 13 through 15 were provided for in the Civil Service Reform Act. However, these have had little effect because of the limited amount of money available for bonuses and increases, the widely varying administrative practices, and the apparent favoritism in bonus awards in some agencies. A contributing difficulty was the development of service-wide appraisals based on a system of performance standards. The net effect of all these factors on civil service morale was not good. The lesson, then, is that compensation is a secondary incentive; the primary one is total cultural acceptance of a high-performance bureaucracy.

The Civil Service Reform Act

This conference necessarily draws renewed attention to the Civil Service Reform Act of 1978 and to questions already under active consideration in Washington. Has the act encouraged improvements in the American higher civil service? Are amendments necessary or feasible? Can the act be more effectively implemented?

This law was a path-breaking statement of policy. For the first time a comprehensive statutory foundation was put under executive personnel management. The act established a Senior Executive Service and provided for how its members would be appointed, compensated, appraised, assigned, developed, and removed. More specifically the act provided for flexibility in assignments, planned mobility as a means of executive development, and bonuses in the SES and merit pay in the next lower executive levels.

What have been the results of the act, as nearly as we can judge them at this time? Although functioning without signs of breakdown, the SES has been a disappointment to many of its members and to many friendly observers. Motivation and morale within the SES have been bad, although mainly for reasons outside the scope of the Civil Service Reform Act. These include limitations and inflexibilities of the salary system; the tendency of political leaders to speak disparagingly of public employees; poor leadership and performance by some presidential appointees, at least as perceived by SES members; severe budget cuts and program reverses; and the unsettling effect of the 1981 change of administration. The mere passage of time and possible future changes in policies and leadership may have some ameliorating effects, but changing the act will do very little for these problems.

One cause of discontent that is clearly within the act's purview are instances of abrupt and allegedly arbitrary reassignments of SES members to obviously unacceptable locations or duties. Some such changes are defensible; others do not seem to be. In general, decisions on job assignments and locations are clearly within management's authority and, under normal circumstances, would be consistent with the act's emphasis on flexibility of assignment. But in a few well-publicized cases, job reassignments were used as a device to force resignations. The result was the formal invoking of grievance procedures without any clear resolution of the issues. Better management could serve to avoid such public wrangling and to make reassignments acceptable to career officials.

There are a variety of proposals for amending the act under consideration by the OPM, congressional committees, and employee groups. Those most relevant to the present discussion propose revision of limitations on performance awards ("bonuses") for SES members; drastic amendment of the merit pay provisions for executives just below the SES level; and enactment of stronger protections for executives being removed, demoted, or reassigned. Such proposals, by and large, would have positive effects, but their chances of enactment are very uncertain. Even if they were agreed to by all interested parties, it would be hard to get Congress to give them priority attention. This difficulty is strengthened by the belief of many in both the legislative and executive branches that they may be opening up a Pandora's box in revising the act.

Whether or not the act is amended, the significant point here is that effective use and management of the higher civil service is now mandated and clearly established as part of the law of the land. Much more can be done to take better advantage of its provisions for executive mobility and career development. More progress will be made in some agencies than in others, depending on the attitudes and leadership capacities of the agency head and on the condition of its budget. Broader progress will depend on the attitude of the White House, the OMB, and the OPM. The law is flexible enough to permit policy movement in various directions. The challenge is to achieve and to sustain high-level interest in improving the career service within the broad framework of the 1978 act.

Toward a doctrine of civil service

The United States needs to establish a civil service doctrine that truly recognizes and accepts that an effective bureaucracy is a major element in the nation's governance.

To be sure, the U.S. civil service has long been recognized by law, regulation, and process. It has an important political and economic impact. The deficiency, as perceived in this conference, is the general lack of interest in the subject and the generally low regard in which civil servants are held by typical citizens. A more positive view of civil servants is not so much something to be deliberately managed as something whose evolution is to be encouraged through prolonged, deliberate educational efforts.

A possible initial step would be to hold a broadly based conference to treat the need for and content of a doctrine of American civil service. Such a conference could be made up of reputable political scientists who have studied the bureaucracy, particularly its upper levels, persons designated by the Republican and the Democratic National Committees, representatives from appropriate congressional committees, a few selected media commentators, and representatives of leading commercial and industrial establishments that are recognized as having succeeded in personnel development. If the report of the present conference were used as a base, a pointed conference agenda could be developed. The goal would be to provide wider recognition of the value of an effective career civil service and to promote the view that those who work in such a service are on a par with the top academicians, professional military people, and the recognized leaders of such professions as law and medicine. Consideration might be given to making this the subject of a White House conference, since it is no less important than other topics that have been the basis for such conferences in the past.

Such a conference would almost inevitably include or lead to an evaluation of the quality of the managerial and professional personnel in the American civil service. If research on this topic is needed, some guidance might be found in a 1979 monograph I wrote for the National Academy of Public Administration, "The Quality of Senior Management in Government in the United States." In addition to the research topics suggested there, a study might also be made of the comparative quality of the college graduates who do and do not go into public service: this would help answer the question, "Is government getting the best, the second best, or what?"

Conclusion

The major conclusion that I draw from looking back at this Brookings conference is that in Canada and the participating European countries, the existence, the relatively high repute, and the optimum functioning of a higher civil service of quality are all taken for granted; in the United States, these are things that are yet to be fully recognized or appreciated. It will be a long, slow process for a European-like attitude toward the higher civil service to be institutionalized and supported politically and financially in the United States. It would help if the president and the leading members of Congress and the media would give even a fraction as much emphasis to this matter as they do to, say, economic conditions, disarmament negotiations, or social welfare measures. Civil servants themselves can do relatively little since their efforts would be properly regarded as self-serving. American opinion leaders need to take some remedial steps before there is a major breakdown of our public bureaucracy.

A Comment on the Future of the U.S. Civil Service

HUGH HECLO

A PERSON can draw many different kinds of lessons from reading these reports. One might have to do with organizational machinery. The Canadians, for example, have much to teach the United States about the formal and informal conditions necessary to create a truly senior group of career managers. Anyone inclined to think about career under secretaries in U.S. departments should take a long hard look at the deputy ministers group in Ottawa. Likewise, the Canadian Public Service Commission introduces the heretical idea that one could look to an independent agency of the legislature, not the executive, to secure an effective merit personnel system. Congress as a whole has an immense stake in an adequate higher civil service, but at present there are few institutionalized ways of expressing that interest. There is a great need for creative thought in this area.

Another lesson might be at the level of maxims. For example, if one can generalize from these papers, it seems that in no country is the higher civil service regarded as working very satisfactorily; the times probably do not allow for widely agreed "solutions" to this issue. Or again, the foreign studies suggest that accountable political control of the bureaucracy is not necessarily a function of the number of political appointees in the bureaucracy. In fact the relationship may be inverse. In the world of Washington politics, that is a thought that deserves to be constantly reiterated.

In my view, however, there is one lesson that transcends all others. The problem of the higher civil service is not, fundamentally, a problem of personnel policy. It is a constitutional issue. By constitutional I mean the fundamental rules (written or unwritten) by which a political community organizes itself. Read any of the papers in this volume and ask yourself, what is the role of a French, or British, or German higher civil servant? Of course, the brief space available to the authors does not allow them to provide enough information for a truly complete answer. But in no country can you even begin to seek an answer by referring to the technical formalities that preoccupy personnel experts in the United States. The role and status of higher civil servants is something that flows out of the evolving constitutional understanding in each nation's political history. In some places and times (Canada is again a good example) that evolution may have a guided quality to it, but the point remains the same: a sense of the appropriate duties and responsibilities of the higher civil service depends on constitutional lore.

If you accept this "lesson," it follows that in the United States, the case for a higher civil service simply has never been made. To do so would require arguing some doctrine of appropriate relationships among the different parts of government—among department heads, their personal aides, and career advisers; among all these and the president's staff; and thence to Congress as a whole and its constituent parts. What is the appropriate role of a cabinet secretary, his personal aides, his permanent senior officials, his assistant secretaries, deputy assistant secretaries, and so on? What norms of appropriate conduct guide their interactions? The case for a higher civil service does not emerge naturally out of constitutional history in the United States as it does in other countries. It is a case that (like the Constitution itself) would have to be self-consciously created. To do so would be a profoundly political undertaking next to which the problems of personnel policy would shrink into insignificance.

We Americans have tried to dance around the problem in several ways. One way has been to try to pretend that career personnel have administrative duties separate from policy or political roles. That view is patently unsustainable under any serious concept of a higher civil service. Current attention to "implementation" has merely given a new name to an old set of blinkers. Another dodge has been to translate the problem of a higher civil service into personnel technologies borrowed from the private sector. Today our thinking about the Senior Executive Service is so preoccupied with merit pay, performance appraisals, bonuses, appeal procedures, and all the rest that it would be a wonder should any members of the SES have a serious understanding of what it means to be a higher civil servant. I do not think that the case for a higher civil service can ever be satisfactorily made by reference to the crude, economistic concepts of business efficiency. A higher civil service lives or dies by the perceived legitimacy of its constitutional calling, something the apparitors of performance management can scarcely imagine.

I should immediately add that I am by no means opposed to

many of the current attempts to bring more efficiency into the public sector. But it is a dangerous delusion to think that the self-identity of any true civil service can ever be based on these techniques or on promises of increased efficiency. A recent issue of *Public Management* magazine, the government's official journal on personnel matters, has a picture of cartoonlike figures (with mindless grins, I might add) engaged in a footrace to cross the finish line of performance appraisals. In my view any senior administrator should be insulted by this puerile image of what his life's work is or should be all about. The techniques are secondary. The important question is who manages them and in accord with what concept of public service.

As a political community we do not know if we want a higher civil service, and we certainly do not know what concept of such a service we prefer. Even the government itself is mindless on the subject. If you doubt that, consider the way the government invests in training senior careerists. The government's own central training facility, the Federal Executive Institute, nearly went under a few years ago. The curriculum it teaches varies with the personal proclivities of a shifting collection of academics, almost none of whom has had experience at the highest levels of government. I respect the efforts made by the overworked staff at the FEI, but that cannot dispel the fact that the federal government has never made a serious commitment of financial or intellectual resources to its own civilian (as opposed to military) training facilities. Insofar as there is high-level training offered for government's most senior managers, it is largely contracted out to places like Harvard's Kennedy School. The striking thing to me about these arrangements is how little the government has to say about the content that it desires in these courses. The government speaks volumes about the contracting procedures that must be followed, but it stands virtually mute in terms of what it wants its senior officials to know and to be. I would argue that this is because the government as such simply does not know what it wants of its higher civil service.

No doubt I am old-fashioned, but even the current terminology of "public management" gives me problems. We hear a great deal more today about training public managers and very little about training civil servants. The way we use words does matter, I think, and the two labels conjure up rather different images. A public manager is a task-oriented achiever of goals; a civil servant is an official in service to the state and public. A public manager thinks about an organization as a kind of ahistorical vehicle for meeting certain goals; a civil servant lives in a world of institutions with historically derived identities and distinctive capacities. A public manager does a job; duties are defined by the managerial task at hand. A civil servant occupies an office; his duties extend beyond any given task and are derived from a shared concept of office. To a public manager, understanding context is simply a means to make better calculations for accomplishing a goal. To a civil servant, understanding context is an end defining the larger responsibilities of office.

I do not think we will get very far by trying to copy particular foreign systems. But I do not think we will get anywhere at all unless we try to deal seriously with the constitutional problem of designing a version of a higher civil service fitted to our own particular needs. Time may be short. The prospects for anything like a higher civil service seem to be deteriorating rapidly in the United States. Public employees are increasingly being seen—and seeing themselves—as just one more special interest group. There is an important segment of opinion on the political right that would prefer to see a less effective rather than a more effective domestic government in Washington. To that group, including many members of the current administration, the legitimacy and morale of the bureaucracy is and should be undermined.

If that sounds provocative, I mean it to be. There are many gentlehearted people who do not realize that a major confrontation is under way as to what kind of government we are going to have in the United States. I do not know of any other developed nation in which the executive management of the government's senior civil service is left to the tender mercies of temporary political appointees. Thinking about the experience of the past twenty years or so leaves me in no doubt: political appointees are unfit managers of our career personnel systems.

First, they are too distracted. Political appointees are inevitably preoccupied with disposing of current business. The best talents of an administration are devoted, as they should be, to the most pressing issues of the day. Civil service issues devolve to the superficial attention of third- and fourth-string appointees.

Second, political appointees are simply uninterested. Effective management of the higher civil service is of immense long-term importance. But nothing that is done will have very much effect during an appointee's own short time in office. Most appointees behave exactly as you and I would if faced with the same incentives: they exploit careerists and do little to build career institutions.

Finally, political appointees are too ignorant to manage career personnel systems. It is an ignorance created by a lack of information about the people and processes at work under them. Assessments of merit, to be realistic, depend on sustained experience in dealing with the people involved and not on mechanical indicators of performance. Short-timers are likely to be more impressed by those who deal conspicuously with problems (sometimes of their own creation) than by those who are truly meritorious, that is, officials who anticipate and head off problems before they need top political attention.

I believe that if we are ever going to have a higher civil service, it will have to be one managed by career officials who are directly responsible to the president and Congress. But we can never have that until there is some shared understanding about the duties and responsibilities we expect of our higher civil service. Everything else is secondary.

Conference Participants

with their affiliations at the time of the conference

Charles Bingman *Senior Executive Association*

Colin Campbell, S.J. *Georgetown University*

James D. Carroll *Syracuse University*

Sir Kenneth Clucas *Former permanent secretary,*
 U.K. Department of Trade

Thomas de Yulia *House Committee on the Post Office and Civil Service*

Alfred Diamant *Indiana University*

Yehezkel Dror *Russell Sage Foundation*

Peter Durant *U.S. Office of Personnel Management*

James W. Fesler *Yale University*

A. Lee Fritschler *Brookings Institution*

Edward Gallas *Organization of Resources Counselors*

Nesta Gallas *City College of New York*

Edie Nan Goldenberg *University of Michigan*

Bernard Gournay *Conseiller Maître à la Cour des Comptes*

Hugh Heclo *Harvard University*

Rosslyn S. Kleeman *General Accounting Office*

Charles H. Levine *University of Kansas*

Charles McC. Mathias, Jr. *U.S. Senate*

Renate Mayntz *University of Cologne*

James M. Mitchell *Brookings Institution*

Frederick C. Mosher *University of Virginia*

Paul E. Peterson *Brookings Institution*

Michael Pitfield *Canadian Senate*

William Plowden *Royal Institute of Public Administration*

Nelson Polsby *Roosevelt Center for American Policy Studies*

John Post *Brookings Institution*

Edward F. Preston *White House Office*

Bruce L. R. Smith *Brookings Institution*

109

Elmer B. Staats *Harry S. Truman Scholarship Foundation*

David T. Stanley *Brookings Institution*

James L. Sundquist *Brookings Institution*

Charles Vallee *Ecole Nationale d'Administration*

William B. Welsh *American Federation of State, County, and Municipal Employees*